THE ART OF
BASKET-MAKING

A BASKET-MAKER AT WORK.

AN INTRODUCTION TO THE
ART OF
BASKET-MAKING

BY

THOMAS OKEY

Quin tu aliquid saltem potius, quorum indiget usus,
Viminibus mollique paras detexere junco ?
VIRG. — *Ecl.* ii, 71-2.

THE BASKETMAKERS' ASSOCIATION

Originally published by Sir Issac Pitman & Sons, Ltd.

This reprint published 1986 by
The Basketmakers' Association
Millfield Cottage
Little Hadham
Ware, Herts SG11 2ED
England

Distribution Address:
12 Charlton Village
Wantage, Oxon OX12 7HE
England

ISBN 0 9511110 0 0

Printed in Great Britain by
The Thetford Press Ltd, Thetford, Norfolk

To

THE WARDENS AND COURT OF ASSISTANTS

OF THE

ANCIENT & WORSHIPFUL COMPANY OF BASKET-MAKERS

OF THE CITY OF LONDON

THIS LITTLE WORK

BY

THE DESCENDANT OF TWO UPPER WARDENS

IS RESPECTFULLY DEDICATED

FOREWORD.

SEVERAL times during this century basketmaking has faded to obscurity, rising to meet the demands of two world wars, and more recently, of renewed respect for traditional skills. Thomas Okey, writing in 1912, perceived its lowly status, and aimed to delay its demise. He was then over sixty, and had been a basketmaker (apprentice, journeyman and Master) all his days. Despite the privation in the East End of London at that time, he had enjoyed and enriched his life by the acquisition of a remarkable virtuosity in modern languages, and a thirst for history and literature. Societies were soon asking him to lecture and teach, and publishers to write and translate. He supported moves for educational and social reform, and world peace, and he travelled in the company of friends such as William Morris, Bernard Shaw, Arnold Toynbee, and many others whose art or philanthropy have made them famous.

On his own admission, he was never happier than when thus occupied, in his spare time, without any thought of personal gain. These achievements led to his second career, for which, ever modest, he was sought out at the turn of the century, and later, widely honoured. He accepted the first Chair of Italian Studies at Cambridge in 1919, yet never lost touch with his origins, examining Basketry for the City and Guilds of London Institute until the age of eighty.

In reprinting this book, the Basketmakers' Association hopes as Professor Okey did, to promote active basketmaking, with all its rewards, by providing a source of traditional techniques, for which the author received the Honorary Freedom of the Worshipful Company of Basketmakers. Acknowledgements are due to the Company for permission to use an early coat of arms, and grateful thanks for encouragement in the re-issue of the text.

E. M. Hardcastle 1986

PREFACE.

THE aim of this little book is not to turn out expert basket-makers—for which considerable aptitude and workshop training are necessary—but rather to indicate some governing principles of the art suggested by the writer's experience of a score of years as apprentice and journeyman and a quarter of a century as employer ; to give elementary instruction in the preparation and nature of material, in terminology and methods; to act as a guide to beginners, and to afford practical information to County Councils and other teaching bodies as to the plant and accommodation required for the institution of classes in basket-work. Little is done officially to foster the craft in this country. We have nothing comparable to the National School of Basket-work established by the French Government at Fayl-Billot ; to the Royal School of Basket-work at Noordwolde in Holland ; to similar institutions at Heinsberg and other places in Germany ; to the sixteen schools in Austria-Hungary and others in the Czech provinces ; to the Federal School at St. Gall in Switzerland. Apart from its economic importance and the stimulus it would give to the demand for one of the most profitable of agricultural products, the art of basket-making affords an admirable means of training in manual dexterity. No minor art practised in modern times is so literally a handicraft ; none in which the action of hand and eye on form and structure is so direct. Without help from mould or shape, with but a knife and a bodkin, the worker has to wrest a handful of crooked, stubborn, willow rods into symmetry of texture and beauty of form.

An attempt to teach so essentially practical a handicraft as basket-work from a book, and by one who has been more used to manual demonstration than to literary exposition, must needs be imperfect, and indeed *is*

vii

probably more imperfect than need be. No written or even oral instruction, no class tuition, can adequately supply the priceless training of a workshop. Far different is the position of a learner sitting once a week for an hour or two in a class-room among other learners all fumbling to attain to some command of their material, from that of one in a workshop, surrounded by an atmosphere of craftsmanship and amid masters of their craft, each striving in that emulation, often unconscious, which obtains when men are working together, men whose every stroke is an incentive to perfection. There, almost insensibly, he progresses in the mystery of his art and absorbs its spirit ; there he is drawn forward even as one who runs a race is drawn forward by the pace-makers. If the writer dare trust his own experience, the increase of literacy, the decay of apprenticeship, the shorter working hours, characteristic of modern times, while they have resulted in a higher average level of workmanship, have produced fewer outstanding and remarkable craftsmen ; men whose names were famed in every workshop, who could work, or play, when they chose, and take a plank where they chose—the Michael Angelos and Raphaels of their obscure and lowly craft.

If this first essay affords any warrant for further development of the subject it is hoped to follow it with a second which shall treat of the higher branches of the art, of some of its more modern methods where it encroaches on the art of the cabinet-maker, and where, often, halting craftsmanship in a hurry is helped along with the aid—*horresco referens*—of hammer and nails, unstructural decoration patched on with tacks, and surfaces daubed with aniline dyes.

In conclusion I have to thank the Society of Arts for permission to use a few sentences and an illustration from an article written for their Journal in January, 1907, and to invite suggestions for the improvement of my book in the event of its reaching a second edition.

THOMAS OKEY.

CONTENTS.

BASKET-MAKING.

CHAPTER I.

INTRODUCTORY.

BASKET-MAKING is the most primitive of the arts. In neolithic times, as surviving tribes of American Indians prove, the basket-maker met the chief requirements of daily life. With no other tools than a sharp flint and a pointed bone, the various materials to hand—rush, willow, sedge, grass, bark, fibre, roots—were prepared and wrought with the aid of teeth and hands, by early ,man, and especially by early woman, into utensils of daily use. From the cradle wherein the papoose was rocked to sleep in a home which was a great thatched basket, to the coffin wherein the brave, his warfare over, was laid to rest in mother earth's bosom, the art of the basket-maker was the chief domestic industry. The toys of primitive man were of basket-work ; he ate from a flat basket and drank from a round one ; the grain which he fed on was winnowed and ground in a basket ; his fish and game were trapped in baskets ; his water was fetched and heated, and his food cooked, in a basket ; he rattled his bone dice in a basket ; his canoe was a basket, and when he wandered he carried his belongings in a basket. Until the advent of the white man, the American Indian had no other vessels, and the number and excellence of her baskets—often of most exquisite form and decoration— were the measure of the squaw's status in her tribe.

Nor have methods changed appreciably since historic times. The baskets made to-day by Nubian women at Wady Halfa are exactly matched by representations of

baskets on Egyptian Pyramids, and baskets found in
Egyptian tombs are constructed with exactly the same
strokes as we use in European workshops to-day—fitch
and pair, plait and track, rand and slew. When travelling
in Galicia a few years ago the writer saw in general use
among Spanish peasants primitive ox-wains with basket
bodies, live axles and solid wheels such as are carved on
Hadrian's Column at Rome.

Basket-work has been the begetter of all the textile
arts ; the basket mould was used by the potter before
the invention of the potter's wheel and the earlier designs
in ceramic ware and in architecture are derived from
basket originals. The venerable antiquity of the art in
this country is emphasised by the old English words
which survive in its quaint and expressive terminology.
The Chaucerian " wad," meaning a bundle, is used by
the basket-maker to-day in exactly the same sense as it
was used by the father of English poetry ; the word
" bodkin " is used, not in the modern sense, but in the
Shakespearean sense of a sharp piercing instrument.
The terms, " Luke, Threepenny, Middleboro," and similar
curious appellations, even the very word Basket itself,
whose etymology is unknown, all point to the great
antiquity of the art. All the learned lucubrations in
encyclopædias, relating Basket to the Latin *bascauda*.
and supported by classic quotations from Martial and
Juvenal, may be dismissed on the authority of the best
lexicographers, such as Sir J. A. H. Murray and Professor
Skeat.

Roughly the art of basket-making may be reduced to
two primitive types :—(1) A core of grass, sedge, fibre,
rush, willow or cane, lapped round with a strip or skein
of similar material, and coiled upon itself in spiral or
elongated coils, each outer coil being laced on to the inner
one as the work proceeds. Fig. 1 reproduces the bottom
of a round basket of this type, found in an Egyptian

FIG. 1.

tomb whose age is counted, not in centuries, but in milleniums.[1] (2) The textile type, in which a series of radiating or parallel rods of material, either entire or cleft into skeins, are filled in by working other rods or skeins alternately over and under, or before and behind them : it is with this second type that we shall be concerned.

Basket-making is essentially a handicraft. It has escaped the application of machinery, and requires for its practice few tools and appliances and small capital. The indigenous and traditional material used from time immemorial by the English basket-maker is the common osier or willow rod in its green, brown (dried) or peeled state. Rods of cane have been imported and used for centuries, and still are increasingly used in this country, and the old Fellowship of Basket-makers in the City of London included those who practised the " art, trade or mystery of Kaine working." In the Far East this material and bamboo are predominantly used by the native basket-maker ; there, where the material is indigenous, is the true home of cane work, and there, with its own traditional methods, it attains its highest artistic development. In Great Britain cane is an exotic material and is worked by the British basket-maker on the same methods as willow. In this Manual, therefore, I shall be chiefly concerned with the species of osier or willow—*Salix viminalis*, *S. triandra* and *S. purpurea*, with their many varieties and hybrids—cultivated by British and Continental growers in places known to us as osier beds, dealing with cane[2] as a subsidiary material. The learner who desires fully to master the craft should begin on willow : he will thereby become the better worker in cane, whereas if he be trained on cane the manipulation of willow will be beyond him.

---

[1] From the collection of R. Mond, Esq., J.P., of Sundridge, Kent.

[2] Where not otherwise specified, " cane " includes both *whole* and *pith* cane.

CHAPTER II.

MATERIAL AND ITS PREPARATION.

(1) Osiers, or willows,[1] comprehensively known to him as "rods," are roughly divided by the basket-maker into "Osier" and "Fine"; the former, consisting of the full-topped and coarser varieties, are chiefly used for common, heavy work; the latter, the lither, tougher, fine-topped sorts, are used for finer work. When cut from the heads in the "bed" the rods are known as "Green whole-stuff," and when sorted into sizes and cured (dried) they are designated "Brown"; when peeled they are termed "White," and when boiled before they are peeled, and thus dyed a rich golden brown from the tannin in the bark, they are called "Buff." Normally the rods are of one year's growth but two-year and three-year-olds are supplied as "Sticks."

(2) Brown rods are sorted[2] in the London District and in the Home and Eastern Counties, approximately into the following sizes—

Luke	from 3 ft. to 4 ft. 6 in.
Long Small	above 4 ft. 6 in. to 5 ft. 6 in.
Threepenny ,,	5 ft. 6 in. to 6 ft. 6 in. or 7 ft.
Middleboro ,,	7 ft. to 8 ft.
Great ,,	8 ft. to 9 ft.

(3) White and Buff Rods are sorted into

Tacks	from 2 ft. 6 in. or 3 ft. to 3 ft. 6 in.

[1] For information respecting the cultivation of willows, see articles by Mr. W. P. Ellmore and the present writer published in the Journal of the Board of Agriculture for April, June and October, 1911, and February and July, 1912.

[2] The roughest of the rods are generally thrown out during sorting, especially from stuff intended for buff or white, and sold as Brown Ragged at the price of Luke. Ragged is used for bottoming and covering of coarse work and sometimes when "shripped up"—i.e., most of the side shoots cut off—for staking.

Small   from   3 ft. 6 in. to 4 ft. 6 in.
Long Small   ,,   4 ft. 6 in. to 5 ft. 6 in. or 6 ft.
Threepenny   ,,   5 ft. 6 in. to 6 ft. 6 in. or 7 ft.
Middleboro   ,,   7 ft.   to 8 ft.
Great [1] (if any) ,,   8 ft.   to 9 ft.

(4) In the Midlands, Green stuff is sorted into Hullings (4 ft. and under) and Rods (above 4 ft.), and other local terms obtain in various parts of the country. Buffing is mostly practised in the Midlands and the stuff is drafted into sizes—

No. 1 (the longest) down to 6 ft.
,, 2 from 6 ft.   ,,   5 ft.
,, 3   ,, 5 ft.   ,,   4 ft.
,, 4   ,, 4 ft.   ,,   3 ft.
,, 5 ⁻   3 ft. and under.

If the stuff runs very small, a No. 6 is drafted 2 ft. and under. Nos. 1 and 2 are sometimes termed Skein rods and Small Skein rods. In this book the Metropolitan terms will be used.

(5) In the Home Counties and in Berkshire, Cambridgeshire, Huntingdonshire, Norfolk and Suffolk, growers sell brown and white by the *Bolt* (white in loads of 80 bolts) of 40 in. girth measured 8 to 12 in. up from the butts ; other counties have their own peculiar gauges. In the Midlands and the North stuff is sold by weight. However the purchase may be effected, first-hand prices will range, for white, from 2d. per lb. for the largest to 3½d. or 4d. for the smallest ; for buff, from 2½d. or 3d. to 6d. or 8d. ; brown, from 1d, to 1½d. Foreign willows (white) are imported chiefly from France, Belgium, Germany and Holland; the last named, being the coarsest is sold at about £14 the ton. These and all following prices vary according to the season and to supply and demand in the markets, and refer to pre-war times.

[1] Often supplied from two-year-old stuff.

(6) Green stuff is sometimes used during the season, especially for slath rods, banding, tying and handling ; it should be used " clung," *i.e.*, partially dried.

(7) *Cane* (*whole*).—Whole cane is sold in bundles of various lengths and substance ranging from about 12 to 16 ft. in length and in diameter from about 4·5 to 8 millimetres. It is classed, according to quality, as Short-Nature, the best and kindest ; Mackerell-back, a medium quality ; and Squeaky, the hardest and heaviest ; assorted small cane of this last quality is sold as Pottery Cane. Prices average from about 2d. to 3½d. per lb. It is used for articles, such as coal baskets and rubbish baskets, which are subjected to exceptionally hard usage, and for upsetting, footing, handling and banding and other parts of willow work where wear and tear are greatest.

(8) *Cane* (*Chair*).—Chair cane is the flinty skin of whole cane made into skeins for bottoming chairs ; it is also used by the basket-maker and sold as Dull, Glossy and Black in four sizes of varying widths, at prices ranging from about 2s. to 2s. 6d. per lb.

(9) *Cane* (*Pith*).—Sometimes known as Pulp Cane, this is of comparatively recent introduction from Germany, and is made by drawing the central pith (after the chair cane has been removed) through cylinders into rods of varying diameters, which are standardised according to Trade numbers ranging from No. 1, about 1·5 millimetres, to No. 16, about 5 millimetres in diameter. Smaller sizes, 0, 00, 000, are supplied for extra fine work. Flat pith cane is also sold of varying substance.[1] The chief defect of this material is the absence of an outer skin and its consequent ragged, dull and coarse surface : it lacks the beautiful silky texture of the skin of the peeled

---

[1] All these materials may be obtained of Mr. Suabedissen, of 7, Mallow St., Old St., London, E.C., who will also supply sample cards of the standardised sizes.

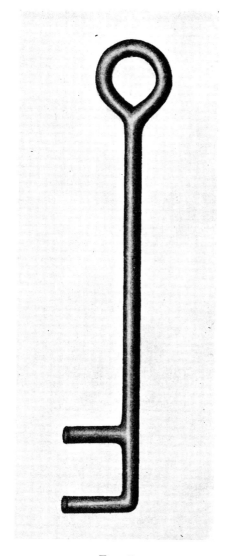

Fɪɢ. 2.

willow. Pith cane is, however, facile of manipulation, and lends itself admirably for use by children, women and home workers generally, as well as the professed basket-maker, by whom it is largely used for wicker furniture, luncheon and other baskets, either alone or combined with willow. The defect alluded to may be to a certain extent remedied by singeing and varnishing.

(10) *Plaits of Raffia, Rush and Straw.*—Ready-plaited material of this nature is also sold to the " fancy-basket " maker, but its use is to be deprecated. When the plait forms part of the integral structure, as in the case of true rush or straw baskets, its use is legitimate, but since the unit of basket-work is the single cane or willow rod, or rush, or skein, the use of ready-made plaits as units is inartistic, and moreover it gives the work a " gouty " aspect.

(11) *Split Cane.*—Whole cane split down the middle and shaved by the shop knife is also used for purposes other than staking, such as siding, bottoming, covering, etc., and also for lapping handles.

CHAPTER III.

TOOLS.

(1) THESE for the beginner who confines himself to simple round or oval work are of the simplest :—A shop knife, a bodkin, and a pair of shears will suffice. The full kit (Fig. 3), however, consists of—

    a. A Shop Knife   costing 1s.[1]
    b. A Picking Knife   ,,   10d.
    c. Two or three Bodkins   ,,   9d. to 1s. 9d.
    d. Shears   ,,   4s. to 5s.
    e. An Iron   ,,   1s. 9d.
    f. A Commander   ,,   2s.
    g and *h.* Cleaves, three-way and four-way, 1s.
    k. A Shave   5s. 6d.
    l. An Upright[2]   7s.

A small mallet, a leaden weight, a rigid yard-measure, sponge, greasehorn, pincers, tool box on which he may sit, are necessary accessories to the full equipment of a basket-maker.

(2) *Plant and Appliances.*—These, too, are inexpensive, and consist for each worker of a plank, usually of elm, about 5 ft. 6 in. by 2 ft. or 2 ft. 6 in. This is raised a few inches above the ground, or floor of the workshop, by

---

[1] A shoemaker's knife at half the cost will serve equally well. The form of this traditional tool dates back to the time when the ordinary workman did not use shears, but cut off his sticks by laying them on the blade of his shop knife, which he held at an angle on the plank, and by pressure of his foot jerked the ends off. Shears are now almost universally used.

[2] An older, and in some ways a superior, form of Commander, known as a " Dog," is still is use—Fig. 2. All these tools (except the Dog) may be obtained in London of J. Buck, 56 Holborn Viaduct. Similar tools may be had in the Midlands of J. Moss, Warrington, and T. Bloor, Leicester.

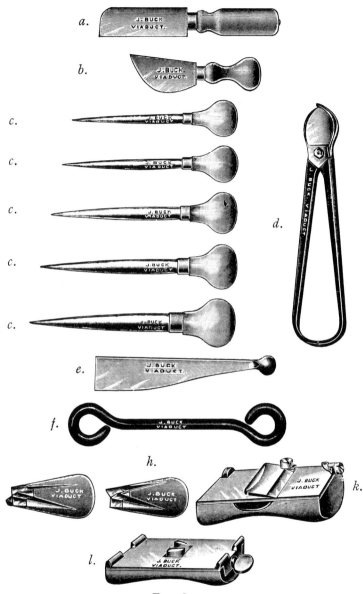

a.

b.

c.

c.

c.

c.

c.

d.

e.

f.

h.

g.

k.

l.

Fig. 3.

loose bricks or other supports. A Lap-board : this may be made by any rough carpenter from a deal board and a piece of quartering, and should be about 2 ft. 9 in. or 3 ft. long by 20 or 24 in. wide, the quartering about 3 in. deep. In the frontispiece a Lap-board is seen in use with the work upon it. Square workers will also require a Square Block (one for each group of two workers). This may be made from two pieces of any heavy, close-grained quartering, 3 ft. or 3 ft. 6 in. long by 3 in. wide and 2½ in. deep, laid side by side, through which two long thumb-screw bolts are run about 6 in. from the ends ; these screw into a plate fixed into the outer of the two members of the block, so that it may be loosened or tightened at will by turns of the screw. The screws should run through the wider axis of the block, which, when closed up, will therefore measure 6 in. across and 2½ in. deep, and will stand firmly on the plank (Fig. 4).

(3) A small and not very efficient block is sold for cane-pith workers by Mr. Suabedissen, the thumb-screws being run through the narrower axis of the block which thus loses in stability and does not resist so well the pull of the work. The tendency to warp has been met by an intrusive centre thumb-screw.

(4) Troughs, tanks or pits for soaking stuff must also be provided. Galvanised iron tanks fitted with inside flanges for holding wooden sinkers in position, are now in general use. A shop-pot, or small shallow vessel for water, is placed in the workshop.

CHAPTER IV.

(1) THE due preparation of material is highly important, and the neglect of this essential preliminary a fertile source of bad work, especially among amateurs. An extraordinary amount of time and care are expended by primitive basket-makèrs in the collection and preparation of their materials, and although accurate knowledge of the periods necessary for soaking and mellowing the various sizes and qualities of willows or cane now in use can only be gained by experience, the following rough table will be found approximately effective—

(2) *Brown Rods.*

Luke should be soaked from two to three days ;
Long Small, three to four days ;
Threepenny and Middleboro, four to five days ;
Large Ragged and Great one week ;

or, if two tanks only be available, the Luke and Long Small may be soaked from three to four, and the larger sizes from five days to a week.

(3) *White and Buff Rods.*—These will require more careful timing.

Tacks may be soaked from one quarter to half an hour.
Small and Long Small, from half to one hour.
Threepenny and Middleboro, from two to three hours.
Great, from three to four hours. Skeins should be merely dipped.

(4) In every case the stuff, when taken from the water, should be laid down in a sheltered place for a night or for some hours to mellow, care being taken not to prepare more white or buff than is needed for one or two days' work. White and buff willows are peculiarly liable to

16

Fig. 4.

turn " greasy " and lose colour if they lie too long unused. Any white or buff stuff left over when the work in hand is finished should be spread out to dry before being stored away for future use. Temperature and the density of the material have also to be considered, for it will be found that longer soaking will be necessary in cold than in warm weather, and that the relative softness or hardness of the variety of the willow will also have a bearing on the time required. Brown rods when watered will keep in condition for a week or more.

(5) *Cane (whole)*.—

Short Nature should be soaked three or four hours. Mackerell-back and Squeaky a whole night.

(6) *Cane (Pith)*.—The smaller sizes should be dipped, the medium, left in the water some few minutes, the largest some hours according to size and density. In all cases cane should be left to mellow in a sheltered place or under a damp cloth.

CHAPTER V.

TERMINOLOGY.

(1) THE engraving (Fig. 5), here reproduced by per mission of the Society of Arts, is of a basket made by the writer to illustrate the chief terms used in common basket-making. They have been in use from time immemorial by professional basket-makers and are applicable to all kinds of material.

(2) It will be seen that the *Slath* is formed by a *Pair* of rods, which, having first bound the six *Bottom-Sticks* together, serve to open them out by being worked alternately over and under each other. When the *Bottom*, by the successive insertion of pairs, has been filled up to the required diameter, the ends of the Sticks are cut off and *Stakes* are inserted alongside each Stick and then *pricked up* to form the rigid fabric of the side. The *Stakes* are then set firmly in their places by an *Upsett*, *i.e.*, three rounds of *Waling*—a *Wale* being three or more rods worked alternately over and under each other. *Bye-stakes* having been inserted between each pair of stakes a round of *Fitching* is then put on—a *Fitch* being two rods worked alternately under and over each other ; above the fitch follows a round of Waling. The next section is formed by a *Rand*—one single rod worked alternately in front of and behind each Stake. The Randing is then followed by another Wale and that by a *Slew*— two or more rods (in this case three) worked together alternately in front of and behind each Stake. The whole is finished by an Ordinary Border, formed by laying down the stakes in a manner to be described in detail later (p. 37) and the basket is stood upside down to receive

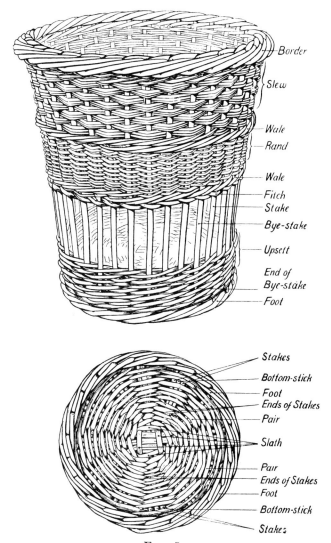

Border

Slew

Wale
Rand

Wale
Fitch
Stake
Bye-stake

Upsett

End of
Bye-stake
Foot

Stakes
Bottom-stick
Foot
Ends of Stakes
Pair

Slath

Pair
Ends of Stakes
Foot

Bottom-stick

Stakes

FIG. 5.

the *Foot*.[1] This is formed by inserting the tops of the rods cut off from the Border alongside each Stake, adding two rounds of Waling, and laying down the Foot-stakes as in an ordinary Border.[2]

(3) Let us now examine more closely the chief material the basket maker will have to deal with. Fig. 6 reproduces the form of a small white willow rod taken at random from a bundle of stuff (Frontispiece). The rod

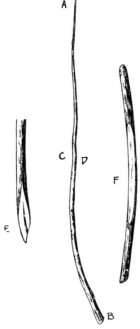

FIG. 6.

has been carefully drawn from nature and it will be observed that the natural rod—like the natural boy— takes much licking into shape. The rod is by no means

[1] The plural of Foot is Foots, not Feet.
[2] For Scalloms see p. 75, Leagues, p. 54.

symmetrical and the worker's skill and aptitude will be measured by his power to wrest this recalcitrant material into a given shape. To the craftsman a simple willow rod has four parts: (*A*) the Top ; (*B*) the Butt; (*C*) the Back ; (*D*) the Belly.

CHAPTER VI.

COMMON SLEWED WORK.

(1) *Round Work.*—Having prepared our stuff, let us attempt a small round slewed basket such as is used to carry a stone jar or a Stilton Cheese. Brown stuff being less expensive and retaining its pliability longer will be preferable to begin with.[1] Some Luke and Long Small will be required or, if white be used, some Osier Small and Long Small.

(2) *Cutting out.*—Sitting on his box, the worker, with his Luke (or Small) to the right-hand of his plant, butts towards him, the Long Small to his left, parallel with his plank, proceeds to cut out his stuff. Let us suppose the basket is to measure 8 in. in diameter and 12 in. deep.[2] Taking his shop knife in his right hand, and selecting four of the largest rods from the stuff to his left, he cuts off from their butts four bottom sticks, 9 in. long, and slypes them—a slype is a long cut—in the middle and on the belly, the cut always being made towards the worker. (Fig. 6, F).

(3) The four rods whence the sticks have been cut and thirteen others, he will now cut out for stakes by two strokes of his knife, the first cut on the belly, the second at right angles to it, either to right or left (Fig. 6, E) straightening each by pressure on the heel of the left hand, and, if using white, rejecting any splitty or crushed rods, which may be laid aside for bottoming.

(4) He then selects two slath rods, about the size of

[1] For the sake of clearer definition the photographic illustrations have been taken from white work.

[2] Unless otherwise specified, dimensions are assumed to be taken inside the basket.

stakes, the smaller of which he cuts out in the manner described above for a stake, and a few smaller rods (also cut out) for slewing up the bottom. Careful economy should be practised in cutting out, as little as possible of the butt being removed, since the butt is the heaviest part of the rod and easily lends itself to waste in chips.

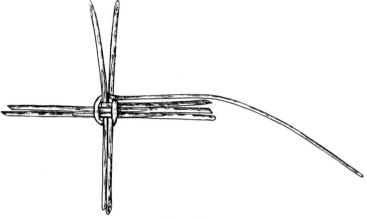

FIG. 7.

(5) *The Bottom.*—Having prepared a round hoop about 9 in. in diameter (compare Fig. 37) and brushed the chips from his plank, the worker, stooping, lays the bottom-sticks cross-wise in pairs, butt and top, on the plank and holding them in position under his feet takes up the larger of the slath-rods, lays it under the sticks, the butt end being to his left and slightly projecting beyond the sticks. This butt end he grasps firmly with his right hand, brings it tightly over to his right, and lays it along-side the two sticks under his right foot, thus forming an odd stick ; then, bringing the slath-rod tightly over and under the sticks, he binds them firmly together, opens the upper pair of sticks and lays it between them (Fig. 7).

He will now take up the second slath-rod,[1] insert it in the aperture to the left of the bend of the first slath-rod (Fig. 8 x; see also Fig. 20 x), and revolving the work under his left foot proceed to open out the sticks by using the slath-rods as a pair. The slath being now finished he

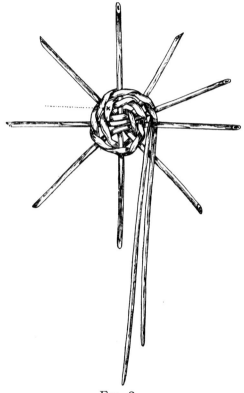

FIG. 8.

slews up the bottom to its required size, the last rod of the slew being worked out and drawn through the work to hold it in its place (Fig. 9). Care should be taken in filling up the bottom to preserve a concave form, thus giving a good " crown " to the bottom when it is reversed.

[1] In very coarse work one slath rod only is used.

(6) The work should be wrought on the stick by pressure of the left thumb [1]—the most important member of the basket-maker's body—and not kinked. The ends of the bottom-sticks are now cut off by the shears and the projecting tops and butts neatly picked off with the picking knife. Cut always down on the stick. The beginner will experience no small difficulty in learning how to work a rod without kinking it, he should therefore allow his instructor to make the first few slaths for him and content himself with filling up the bottom until he is able to obtain some command of his material and learn to work easily in a stooping position—a necessary but unpleasant discipline known in the workshop as "taking his backbone out."

(7) *Staking up*.—Dipping the butt ends of the seventeen stakes in the shop-pot the worker stakes the bottom up by inserting first the odd stake [2] where the bottom-sticks are closest (*i.e.*, alongside the centre of the three formed by the odd stick), then the remainder in pairs one each side of the remaining sticks. Each stake should be driven in, with its belly towards the worker, who grasps the stake tightly with the left hand and slides the right hand down the stake bringing its weight heavily upon the left. Reversing the bottom (Fig. 10) he proceeds to prick up each stake in succession by inserting the point of the shop-knife just beyond the level of the bottom-stick and giving a half turn of the wrist as he bends up the stake in order not to fracture the skin. The stakes are then gathered up into the left arm and the hoop is passed over them.

[1] " The sallow knows the basket-maker's thumb."—Emerson, *May Day and other Poems*. Wherein the transcendentalist poet proves himself to be but an indifferent interpreter of the basket-maker's feelings, for if there is one species of willow his thumb desires *not* to know it is the sallow—the most coarse and unkind of all willows.

[2] A little reflection will explain the need of an odd stake in a slewed basket.

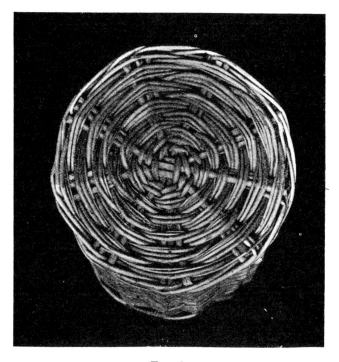

Fig. 9.

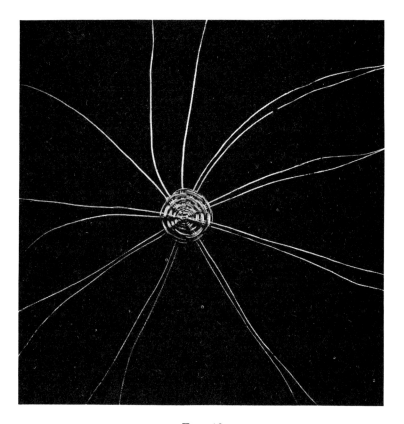

Fig. 10.

(8) *The Upsett.*—Sitting on his plank the worker will level the stakes by a tap of the handle of the shop-knife or the iron, and replace any that may have been broken in pricking up. Selecting and cutting out three upsett-rods, rather smaller than the stakes, he inserts these alongside three successive stakes,[1] beginning at the odd one, and wales each upsett-rod in succession over two and behind one stake (Fig. 9), bringing the turns well down between the stake and the stick so as to bind the whole structure firmly together and set the stakes in their positions, pair by pair. When the upsett-rods[2] have been worked out to their tops the work is placed on the lap-board, and kept from sliding about by a weight inside, or by pinning it to the board with a small bodkin inserted through the middle of the slath, on which it will revolve as on a pivot (frontispiece). Raising the board on his lap he now begins the

(9) *Siding Up.*—The worker, using the Luke (or Small) lying at his right hand, picks up the siding, rod by rod, and lays the slewing in with a three or four rod slew (Fig. 11).[3] When two or three slews have been put on, the Hoop may be removed ; the slews should be made to touch by closing up the work with a sliding drive of the left hand down the stake, bringing the heel of the hand sharply on the slewing.[4] The diameter of the basket should be gauged and kept uniform by the frequent use of the yard stick. As the work proceeds care must be taken : (*a*) to keep the pairs of stakes as far as possible upright, equidistant and symmetrical

[1] Or the last upsett-rod may be simply laid in (Figs. 9, 11, 16).

[2] Very coarse work is sided up without an upsett, or is upsetted with a pair instead of a wale.

[3] The older craftsmen carry the fill-in rod several stakes back, thus going over the work twice, instead of one stake back as in the illustration.

[4] The hand may be protected by a leather covering until the heel hardens.

and the odd stake in its place ; (*b*) to avoid kinking the
stakes ; (*c*) to lay the slew on the stake by pressure of the
thumb of the left hand, while the stake is held in position
by two or three fingers placed behind it. This the tyro
will find no easy matter. The stakes, with diabolical
perversity, will have an obstinate tendency to kink or
splay out into any but the desired position ; the beginner
should therefore get his teacher to upsett for him and
start a few rounds of slewing, himself practising simple
slewing until he attain some command over his material,
patiently and doggedly setting himself to master it and
not let it master him. Let him remember, as I have
already said in my preface to Miss Latter's little manual, [1]
that the ultimate perfection of shape and symmetry of
texture will depend on the more or less perfect idea of
form in the mind of the craftsman and his power to
impress such form on a stubborn material. Every
movement of his fingers will have a permanent effect on
the ultimate form of the basket and no subsequent
pressure will alter it. The result is irrevocable, for it is
impossible to mould afterwards into good form any
article that has been ill-shapen during the progress of the
work. There is nothing for it but to destroy the bad
work and begin over again—a most wholesome discipline.

(10) *The Border.*—Having slewed the basket up to its
required depth, a simple, ordinary border will complete
this part of the work. Beginning at the odd stake, prick
down four consecutive stakes about a quarter of an inch
above the line of the slewing ; lay the first down behind
the second, bringing the top towards you ; lay the
second similarly behind the third, the third behind the
fourth and the fourth behind the fifth. It will facilitate
matters for beginners if they are numbered one to
seven (I, II, III, etc.) with a blue pencil about a foot
beyond the turndown of the border. The tops of the

[1] *Cane Weaving for Children,* by Lucy R. Latter (Pitman).

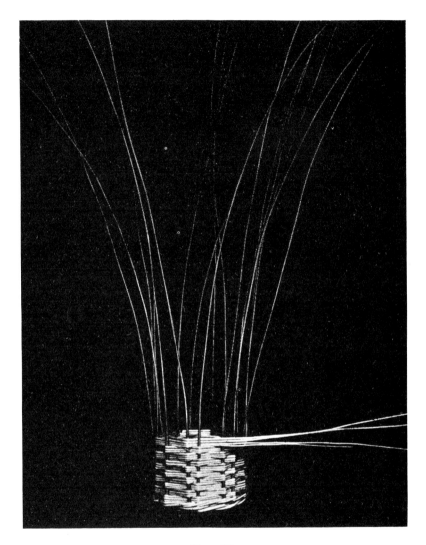

Fig. 11.

four laid down will now project towards the worker. Of these take up the first, loop it in front of the third, fourth and fifth, and lay it behind the sixth. Turn down the fifth stake (this should be done by a slight turn of the left wrist to prevent fracture), and lay it behind the sixth stake and alongside the first, which has now done its

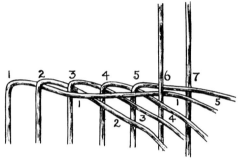

Fig. 12.

work. (Fig. 12: for greater clearness the slewing has been cut away). Take up the second, loop it in front of the fourth, fifth and sixth stakes, lay it behind the seventh, then turn down the sixth behind the seventh and alongside it, which also has done its work. Continue thus until the border is completed as far as the odd stake, when all the stakes will have been laid down save one. The next stroke to be taken up, instead of being laid behind the

Fig. 13.

first stake, is turned down, sharpened (Fig. 13) and crammed down alongside and in front of it. The last remaining stake is now topped, *i.e.*, the top of the stake is cut off, leaving it about a foot in length ; it is then drawn carefully behind the first stake into its place (Fig. 15). Each of the remaining rods, including that just drawn through, is successively crammed down alongside and in front of a stake, and the whole spaces are thus filled up. The crams should be turned down just a little short of the stake alongside which they are to be

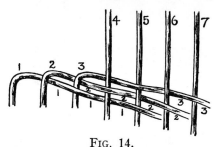

FIG. 14.

inserted, in order to pull the stroke tight as they are driven in (Fig. 17). The projecting tops are now neatly cut off and laid aside for use as slewing in the next basket to be made.[1] If a stake should break in the course of the border another may be pieced in alongside and before it; but this should rarely happen if the stuff has been properly watered and not allowed to dry. Care must be taken to lay in the various strokes of the border firmly without kinking ; nothing is so distressing to the professional eye as a " sore-fingered " border.

(11) *The Running Border.*—This is a still simpler form of border. Number seven successive stakes (Fig. 14).[2] Lay down the first behind the second and again behind the fourth, leaving the end of the rod projecting outwards against No. 5 or turning it inwards behind No. 6. Lay

[1] For variations of this border see p. 96.
[2] The strokes are drawn loosely for the sake of greater clearness. In actual practice they should be thumbed tightly in.

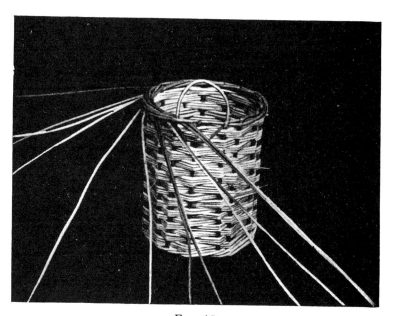

Fig. 15.

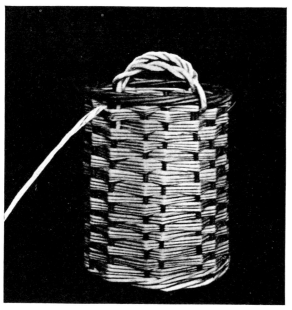

Fig. 16.

Fig. 17.

down the second behind the third and again behind the fifth, and so continue. The border is finished by drawing the last rods into their respective positions, first twisting them to prevent fractures. Cut off the ends of the border rods as before.[1] The border may be deepened by taking an extra stroke or two downwards.

(12) *The Handle—Single.*—One, or two, handles will complete the basket if it is not to be covered. The simplest form is as follows. Select a stout, firm, smooth handle-rod from the Long Small, insert it alongside the odd stake ; top off a small portion ; then, holding the basket between the knees, grasp the handle-rod at the top firmly in the right hand, twist it carefully downwards, while guiding the twist by the left, to the point of insertion in the border, so as to give the rod a rope-like facility of manipulation. Then draw the rod through the slewing under the border until an arc is formed the intended size of the handle. The rod is then reversed and given two (or three) turns on itself, when it will have the appearance of a two-strand rope (Fig. 16, front). It is now taken again under the border and again reversed, when the handle will resemble a three-strand rope (Fig. 16, back) ; draw the top through the turn under the border and cut it off. If cane is used it need not be twisted, the material being flexible enough without. The second handle, if needed, should be put on opposite the first.

(13) *The Double Handle.*—For larger work a stouter and more rigid handle may be formed of two rods. This handle is worked on from the opposite side of the basket, which is held between the knees or, if larger, the handles are put on standing, the basket being held in position by the left foot. The larger of the two handle rods is inserted to the left alongside a stake, the smaller rod to the right alongside a stake at a distance equal to the diameter of the arc of the handle. The first rod is then

[1] See p. 96 for variations in this border.

drawn *untwisted* under the border to the right beyond the stake alongside which the second rod is inserted ; this forms the rigid bow of the handle and is then temporarily dropped.   The second rod is now twisted, and two (or three) turns are taken with it round the bow to the left, care being taken to keep it well twisted and not to deform the curve of the bow ; it is then drawn under the border and an equal number of turns are taken round the bow in the reverse direction, when it is drawn under the border alongside the first (the bow) rod, again reversed, other turns are taken round the bow to the left and the rod, which has done its work, is dropped (Fig. 17).   The first rod is now twisted down to the border, similar turns are taken round the bow with it to the left, where it is looped under the border, gripping the dropped second rod between itself and the former loop ; reversed turns round the bow are then taken to the right, where the rod is drawn through the loops and between the insertion of the second rod and the bow ; or if the bow is not well covered it is again reversed, without being looped under the border, and drawn through the loops to the left and cut off (Fig. 18). This handle may also be formed of cane, which, being used untwisted and therefore of uniform elasticity, is more difficult of manipulation ; the bow will have a tendency to become involved with the turns taken over it, thus deforming the handle.   In Figure 19 I have illustrated a single (three turns) and a double handle (two turns) in cane.

(14) *The Cover.*—If our basket is to be covered—as in a Stilton Basket—the worker will cut out sticks, slath-rods, and slewing as for a bottom, allowing the requisite margin of length on the sticks.   The cover is made on the same principle as the bottom, but the worker should be careful to piece in the butts of the slewing towards him (Fig. 20).   The slewing is finished off with a pair.

Fig. 18.

FIG. 19.

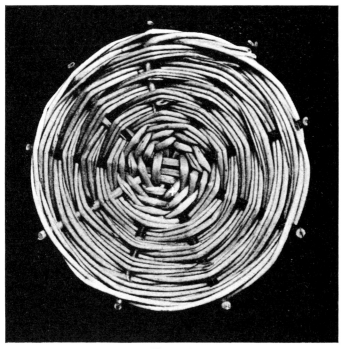

FIG. 20.

(15) Selecting two rods about the size of slath-rods he inserts them alongside and in front of two successive sticks. They are then paired round the slewing until the pairing overlaps the insertion of the rods, the tops are then drawn through the pairing and cut off (Fig. 20). The cover-sticks are now neatly cut off with the shears— not closely as in the case of the bottom, but allowing a margin of half an inch or so from the end of the stick so that the pairing may not slip off (Fig. 20). The cover is tied on with one of the single-rod handles,[1] the handle rod being taken through the cover as well as under the border to form a continuous handle and hinge (compare Fig. 32).

[1] If one handle only is put on, it should be placed over the crams of the border.

CHAPTER VII.

COMMON SLEWED WORK (CONTINUED).

(1) *Oval Work. Cutting-out.*—The simplest form of oval work may next be attempted—say a small packing hamper about 12 or 13 in. long by about 8 in. wide and deep, with a spring or flow of a couple of inches. Stuff as for the round basket above. Cut out as follows :— Six *leagues*—a league is a continuous bottom-stick and stake—seventeen stakes, four slath-rods and some slewing for the bottom. Slype the leagues on the belly near the butts, as in the case of the round basket.

(2) *The Slath.*—Holding the butts of two slath-rods under the right foot, lift up one of them (the left) and lay a pair of leagues, butt and top, between the slath rods, allowing a margin of butt sufficient to form the width of the bottom, say a space of 10 in. between butt and butt ; about 4 in. of the butts of the slath rods should remain clear under the foot to form the end sticks of the bottom. Holding the first two leagues in position with the left foot, proceed to lay in the remaining two pairs of leagues between the slath rods (Fig. 21). Some difficulty may be encountered at first in estimating the relation of the length of the slath to the size of the bottom, but, roughly, in ordinary work the leagues should be laid in so as to occupy about half its required length. The six leagues being laid in, are then held in position by the left foot, and the other two slath-rods are worked in (Fig. 21), the butts being laid under the left foot and also allowed to project about 4 in. The slath-rods at each end are now brought tightly and alternately over and under the projecting butts (Fig. 21). The butts at the ends together with the leagues are then

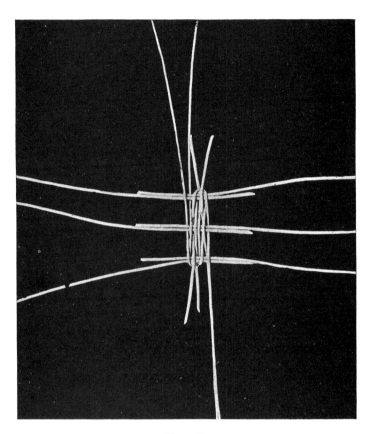

FIG. 21.

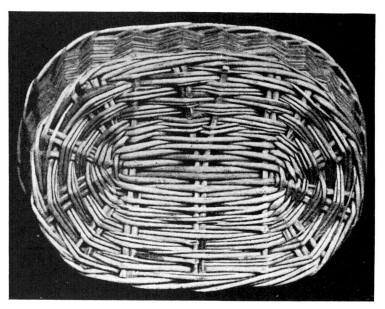

FIG. 22.

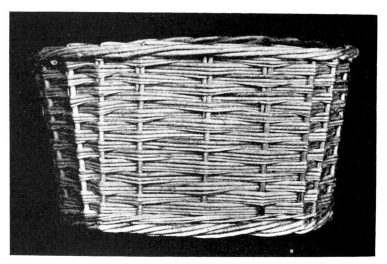

FIG. 23.

opened out by the slath-rods, one pair excepted (Fig. 22) ; the slath rods are worked out ; the bottom is slewed up to its required size and the sticks are cut off, leaving the six leagues in their places.

(3) Any small modification of the proportion between length and width may be made, during the slewing up of the bottom, by piecing in the rods of the bottoming chiefly at the ends or sides as the work proceeds. The relative axes of the oval may also be modified at will by increasing the number of leagues, or sticks if leagues are not used (Fig. 17). It will be seen from Figure 17[1] that, where an even number of pairs of leagues or sticks is used, the centre strokes lie alternate, and not side by side as in Fig. 22. The alternation may be retained in the latter case by piecing in a slip of rod between them. Pairs of bottom-sticks are more generally used for finer work, the obvious structural effect of the league (Latin *liga,* from *ligare* to bind) being to bind the bottom and sides of a coarse slewed basket together so that it may safely carry a heavy packing. Care should be taken to maintain a uniform upward slope of the sides and ends of the bottom so that when staked up it may stand evenly and maintain a good crown. It should also be well shouldered, *i.e.*, well rounded at the four corner curves.

(4) *Staking Up.*—Having prepared an oval hoop rather larger than the oval of the bottom we proceed to stake up in pairs at the ends and shoulders, and in singles at the sides. Then when pricked up there will be, including the leagues, four single stakes at the front, *i.e.*, where the middle pair of leagues has been opened out, and three· at the back (Fig. 23).[2] We now insert our three upsett rods, beginning at the front and at the left shoulder (Fig. 22), and work round to the back, where, the rods

[1] Compare Fig. 24.

[2] Or added strength may be given by inserting pairs of stakes next the shoulder pairs.

being attenuated, we strengthen them by piecing in three additional upsett rods (Fig. 23). The stakes should be set slightly outwards at the ends and shoulders to give the flow, and the pairs of stakes should diverge slightly for the same purpose (Fig. 23). Slew up to the required size, and finish with an ordinary border, beginning at the back.

(5) *The Cover.*—Six cover-sticks and six slath-rods will be required. Placing four of the slath-rods under the right foot, lift up two alternate rods and lay in between them one pair of sticks, butt and top, then, successively, two single sticks and the remaining pair of sticks. Work in the two remaining slath-rods from the left, and take two alternate turns round each end (Fig. 24). Open out the ends by successive pairing 1×1, $1 \times 2 \times 1$, and open out also the pairs of sticks at the shoulders. When the slath is fully opened out, fill up the cover with slewing, and finish off with a pair (Fig. 24) as in the cover of the round basket.

(6) A firmer and more pleasing method of finishing off the covers, especially of the larger size hampers (Fig. 25), known as Tracking,[1] has fallen into desuetude since the advent of modern industrialism, in its haste, intolerant of craftsmanship. The quicker paired finish is now almost universally adopted, and the pair is generally held in position by one or two long bands on the front of the cover as described later (Fig. 26).

(7) *Handles and Ties.*—The cover may be tied on with a single-rod handle at the back, as on a round basket, but, for larger sizes, the handles should be worked on at the ends (Fig. 26) before the border is laid down, care being taken that the handle-rod grips a stake as well as the slewing. Double-rod handles may also be applied to the ends of hampers. The covers of these larger sizes are tied on by inserting two tie-rods alongside two cover sticks.

[1] See pp. 112 and 121 for description of this method.

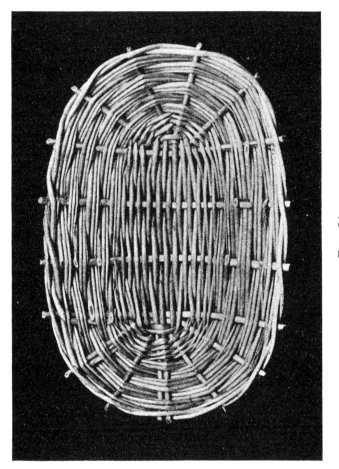

FIG. 24.

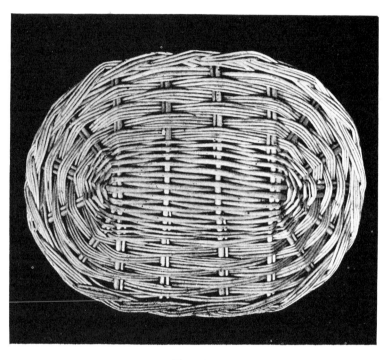

Fig. 25.

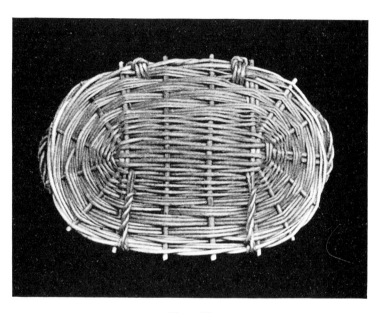

FIG. 26.

Each in turn is then twisted, and, with the aid of the bodkin, drawn thrice through the cover and under the border ; it is finished off by a turn through the tie itself to the right, another turn to the left through the loop thus formed, then drawn through between the tie and the cover and cut off (Fig. 26). The tie-rods should be kept well twisted as the tying proceeds.

(8) Having grasped the simple strokes used in the making of a common slewed basket, and having obtained some command of his material, the pupil may be set to work on larger sizes and stouter stuff, increasing the number of sticks and stakes and adopting a broader treatment. In all the specimens illustrated I have worked the slewing more finely than is usual, or indeed necessary, in common work, but it is well that the pupil should begin on these lines : as he progresses in the practice of the art he will be able to " put the Roman in," as the shop phrase runs for broad and rapid slewing. There is no reason why an alert lad may not learn in the course of one or two winters' tuition [1]—not indeed to become an expert basket-maker—but to make in tolerable style most of the common round and oval work used by fruit and other farmers in this country, such as Bushel Sieves, Currant Sieves, Potato Hampers, etc., for which there is a large demand, increasingly met by foreign supplies. Fruit farmers especially, by engaging youths thus trained, might maintain a permanent staff of hands throughout the year, the winter months, when field work is impossible, being devoted to making up baskets for summer requirements. Little capital is needed ; a barn would serve excellently for a workshop and for storage, and, if in the vicinity of osier-beds, the stuff could be obtained at a minimum cost for carriage.

[1] Preferably in day technical classes, devoting the whole of his time to the work ; if in evening classes at least three or four attendances of two hours weekly should be demanded.

In the report read at the General Meeting of the members of the *Chambre Syndicale des Osiéristes Français* held at Paris, 30th March, 1911, on the state of the basket industry in Belgium, it was stated that in the counties of Tamise, Borheim, etc., 1,200 men were employed in making ordinary white osier work, nearly the whole of which, consisting of fruit baskets, was destined for the English market.[1] One London firm alone, known to the writer, imported during the same year no less than 152,845 fruit baskets, chiefly sieves, from the Continent.

(9) *Oval work continued.*—We may now set about the making of a small slewed arm-basket, 10 in. long by 6 in. wide and deep. We shall require some White Short and Long Small, and a stout Great, or small two-yearling, rod for the handle-bow; and, since an even pair of stakes will be needed in the middle of each side, the odd stick may be relegated to one of the ends, or, if even stakes are used, the slewing may be worked in two alternate slews, begun at opposite sides and one following the other.

Having prepared the stuff, slype six bottom-sticks, cut out twenty-nine stakes and select six slath-rods. Begin with four slath-rods under the right foot and lay in three pairs of bottom-sticks (compare Figs. 24 and 21). Before working in the remaining two slath-rods at the opposite end, lay in a short slip of rod to maintain the alternation of the strokes and then open out the ends and shoulders of the slath as in the cover (Fig. 24). Stake up in pairs, except at the end where the four slath-rods have been opened out into three for the odd stake. Upsett as in the hamper; or, more symmetrically, the upsett may be begun both at front and at back, instead of piecing in at the back. When slewing up the sides, carry the slew over the central pair of stakes (Fig. 27), which pair should

[1] Journal, *L'Union Nationale du Commerce*, etc., Paris, 6th May, 1911, p. 167.

Fig. 27.

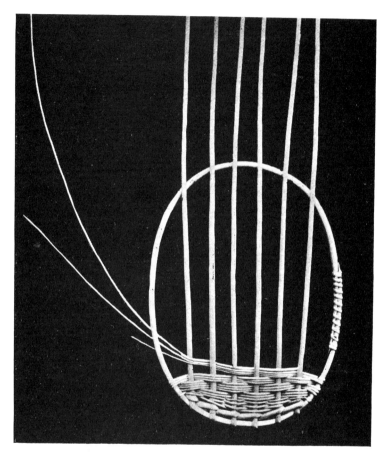

Fig. 28.

be kept even by the insertion of two liners,[1] *i.e.*, two butt ends cut long enough to admit of their being easily withdrawn after the basket has been bordered. Lay down the border behind two stakes and in front of three or four ; the left-hand stake of the handle pairs may be cut off, or pieced back in the place of a dropped stroke. It will be necessary, of course, in finishing the border to draw the last *two* stakes into their places, and to cram in six or seven instead of five last strokes.

(10) *The Cross Handle.*—Having drawn out the liners, take the bow-rod ; sharpen the butt end and insert it down one side between the open pair of stakes (Fig. 27) ; bend it over carefully, without kinking, by pressure of the thumbs, to the required arc of the handle; cut off the top, allowing sufficient length to pass down between the corresponding open pair of stakes at the opposite side (Fig. 27).[2] Select and cut out four firm, long rods rather larger than stakes; top them a few inches, and insert the first to the right of and alongside the bow ; twist it down to the border and take four turns round the bow to the opposite side ; there it should be looped under the border and brought back, with other four turns, over the bow, to the point where it was inserted, the top being temporarily fixed in the slewing to prevent the turns slipping from their position. Insert a second handle-rod opposite the first, twist it, take it four times over the bow, loop it under the border at the opposite side, catching up and holding fast the top of the first rod. Now insert successively the other two handle-rods at opposite sides, take each of them four times forward and backward over the bow, and once under the border, drawing the tops, when their work is done, through

[1] If the centre is a single stake, liners may be inserted each side of it to give place to bow rods for a lapped handle (Fig. 60).

[2] The slype of the bow-rod should be turned inwards. Compare Fig. 55.

the loops to hold them fast (Fig. 27). If the bow-rod should not be well covered and should " grin " through the handling, another small rod may be inserted, twisted, and an extra four turns be taken over the bow to fill up more closely.

If the handling is of fine willow an expert worker will carry the handle rods round the bow and under the border untwisted. This method, however, has the effect, unless the siding is closely and strongly wrought, of wrenching the work out of shape owing to the stronger pull of the untwisted rods. This may to a great extent

Fig. 29.

be counteracted by putting a cross tie from side to side with a pull in the reverse direction, and allowing it to remain until the basket is dry. The sides may also be strengthened by an inch or two of randing on the top. If the basket is to be covered as well as cross-handled the method described on pp. 139, 140 may be adopted.

(11) *Hoops and Scalloms*.—Bottoms and covers may also be made on hoops and scalloms. A stout one or two-yearling hoop is turned to the size and form of the bottom and temporarily held in position by a small rod or skein lapped round the join (Fig. 28). Scalloms for bottom and sides are next cut out by a long slype down the butts on the back (Fig. 29). Those for the bottom are scallomed on by laying the slype of the scalloms against one end of the hoop, at the necessary intervals. Bring the tongue of the first scallom tightly round the hoop and over itself to the left (Fig. 30), where it is held in position

Fig. 30.

by the thumb while the second scallom is laid on ; this, as it is brought round the hoop, grips and holds fast the tongue of the first scallom (Fig. 28). Each succeeding scallom thus grips the tongue of the preceding one and the last tongue is laid against the hoop and held in position by a preliminary rand. The bottom is then slewed (or it may be randed) up (Fig. 28). When the slewing or randing reaches the join of the hoop the lapping is removed, since the work will hold the hoop in position ; for greater security a turn of the slewing or randing

may be taken round the juncture of the hoop. To finish
the bottom, the ends of the scalloms are topped and
twisted ; each is then taken over the hoop and round
on itself with a stroke similar to that of the laying on of
the scalloms ; or the ends may be slyped and turned over
and in.[1] If the cover or bottom be a large one, two
hoop-rods may be used instead of one and lapped at
opposite sides.

The hoop and scallom method is an invaluable one to the
basket-maker, for it enables him to turn his bottom or
cover to any abnormal form—triangular, half-moon, etc.
No self-respecting craftsman will descend to the humiliat-
ing expedient of wooden bottoms, the refuge of the incom-
petent. The stakes for the sides are scallomed on to the
bottom in a similar manner, except that the tongue of the
scallom is usually cut long enough to be gripped by two
successive ones (see p. 80).

(12) *Slewed Work : Square.*—The construction of a
square basket is of the simplest ; to make square work
square is by no means so simple and demands longer
apprenticeship and greater aptitude than either round or
oval forms of basket-work.

(13) *The Bottom.*—The square block will now come
into use and, for large work, the commander or dog.
Let us begin with a small, common square hamper,
say 13 in. long by 10 in. wide and 9 in. deep. Some
Luke, Long Small and Threepenny will be needed, and a
few small two-yearling sticks ; if white stuff be used,
some Osier Small, Long Small, Threepenny and Sticks.
Placing the square block before him across his plank
the worker cuts out with his shears six bottom sticks,
15 in. long,[2] and, having slyped the ends of the stouter

---

[1] The size of the scallom rods in the illustration is exaggerated ;
they should be about half the substance of the hoop.
[2] In the Midlands it is customary to cut the sticks to correspond
with the width of the basket and to increase their number.

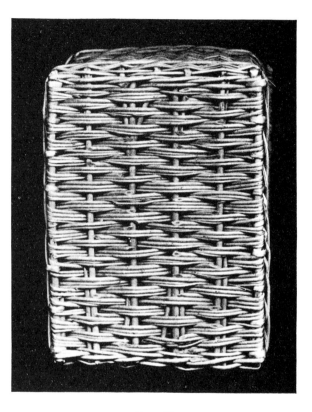

FIG. 31.

sticks so as to render the grip of the block uniform on each, he inserts them in the block alternately, butt and top, chosing the two stoutest for the outside sticks ; the sticks are placed at regular intervals, allowing a small reduction of width for the turns of the slewing over the outside sticks. The block is now screwed up tightly, the bodkin being inserted in the eye of the screw and used as a lever (Fig. 4). The bottom is begun with a pair formed of a stout Threepenny rod (Fig. 4), and is then slewed up to its required length with Long Small ; the butts should be laid in away from the worker, and a margin allowed for the finishing pair (Fig. 31), the last turn of which is crammed in. Here again the tyro will experience no small difficulty in keeping to form ; the outside sticks will have a tendency to be drawn inwards with the pull of the slewing ; to counteract this the outside sticks should be set slightly outwards (Fig. 4) and held firmly with the hand as the slew is turned round them.

(14) Having cut off the top sticks, release the bottom from the block, cut off the lower sticks and pick off the butts and tops of the slewing. The stakes should be cut out from the Threepenny—seven for each end, nine for the front and eight for the back. The fourteen end stakes should be cut out on their *backs* and more sharply pointed than for a round or oval basket ; the seventeen (which are to be scalloms) cut also on their backs and with a long slype (Fig. 29). Having prepared an oval or a square hoop, and sitting on his box with the bottom held between the knees, the butts of the slewing towards him, the worker first stakes up the ends, choosing the stoutest for the corner stakes, which are driven with the aid of the bodkin down the outside bottom stick, the other five being driven in at equal intervals alongside a stake or through the pairs (Fig. 31), or the bottom sticks may be spaced out by driving in short liners.

Gathering the end stakes up into the hoop, the scalloms

are next laid on to the sides, working from right to left.
Having first carefully marked his intervals, the worker
selects the stoutest for the outside, pushes the tongue of
the scallom through the slewing of the bottom, brings
it tightly round and over the stick to the right of the stake,
and then brings it firmly round the stake to the left, thus,
setting the stake upright against the bottom-stick (Fig.
30). Holding the tongue in position, he now lays in a
second scallom which, as it is turned over the bottom-
stick and round the second stake, grips and holds the
tongue of the first scallom in position ; a third scallom
is then laid in, the tongue of which in its turn grips both
the first and the second ; and so all the side stakes are
scallomed on, the tongue of the last scallom being laid
under the first of the end stakes[1] (Fig. 32).

(15) When the side stakes are scallomed on, they are
gathered into the hoop and two or three rounds of upsetting are put on, beginning with the tops at that end
which will allow of the butts of the waling being pieced
in at the front and not at the back (Fig. 32). Since,
however, there will be gaps at the ends corresponding
to the space taken up by the scalloming at the sides, these
gaps should be filled by a small rod either paired or randed
in before the upsett is begun.

The basket is now ready to be slewed up to its required
depth. Here, again, the beginner will have to wrestle with
the recalcitrancy of his material, and the art of keeping
the corners square and the basket shapely will be but
slowly and painfully acquired. The slewing is terminated
by a wale. An ordinary border is laid down and the
work—or " belly " as an uncovered basket is technically
termed—will be ready for the cover.

(16) *The Cover.*—Seven sticks will be needed for the
cover, which is made on the same principle as the bottom

---

[1] Or the whole set of scalloms may be thrust through the
slewing before the tongues are brought round and laid in position.

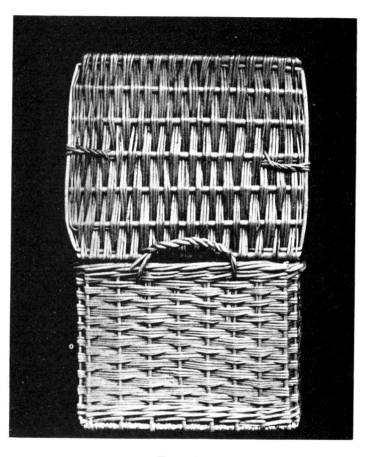

Fig. 32.

except that it need not begin with a pair. It should be carefully adapted in size and shape to the belly, the blunt corners being formed by a narrow rand in the manner shown (Fig. 32). The ends are finished by cramming in stout rods, which are held in position by bands in the centre. The band is made by inserting a rod alongside a stick, topping and twisting it, as for a handle, then taking one turn round the stick a few inches up, two on itself and two round the cram and the randing, before the last turn is taken along its length and the top cut off (Figs. 26 and 32).

(17) *The Handle.*—The cover is tied on with a single handle, the butt of which is inserted alongside a stake (Fig. 32). In larger square hampers, as in oval, the handles are placed at each end under the border, and the cover is swung on ordinary ties (Fig. 57).

CHAPTER VIII.

FITCHED WORK.

(1) THE fitch is one of the most universal and primitive strokes practised in basket-work and has been found in use by natives of lands as far apart as Tasmania, Egypt, the Far East, and North and South America. In England its use is confined to the construction of open or skeleton work, such as waste paper baskets, cages, cabbage crates, prickles (generally used for the transport of empty glass bottles), cradles, shoulder baskets, and numerous other articles of common use ; it is especially efficacious in gripping and firmly holding the stakes in position.

(2) Applied to common round or oval work, it is usual to supplement the stakes with bye-stakes (Fig. 5), which are inserted in the waling of the upsett between the pairs of stakes.[1] This is termed half bye-staking. Square work is full bye-staked—a bye-stake being inserted between each stake—or the stakes may be increased in number and set more closely together.

(3) A fitch (Fig. 33) may be started in two ways : (*a*) with the butts, (*b*) with the tops. (*a*) Having selected two tough, kind rods, the longer is first turned round the bodkin a few inches from the butt and then the turn is taken round the stoutest of the stakes (if the turn is taken direct round the stake a kink may result), or, in the case of square work, round the left-hand corner-stick or stake, beginning at each side. A turn is then taken in front of and behind the next stake, the butt is dropped and the second fitch rod pieced in (Fig. 34). The fitch is then continued until the beginning is reached, where it may be turned into a pair (Fig. 35) or a wale (Fig. 5), pieced and

[1] The slype of the bye-stake should be turned inwards.

84

carried round the fitching; or, if a simple fitch be used, the tops may be crammed in. If the fitch rods become too attenuated before the fitch is carried round, two other rods may be pieced in, top and top, and the double fitching

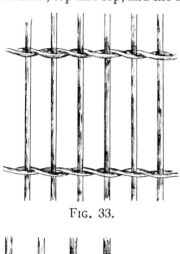

Fig. 33.

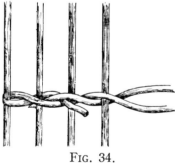

Fig. 34.

continued for a few strokes, after which the tops of the first fitch rods may be dropped and the work continued and finished with the butts of the rods which have been pieced in. If cane is used for fitching, the greater length of the hanks will obviate the necessity of any piecing.

(b) Begin with the tops of the fitch-rods direct on the stake and work them in for a few strokes (Fig. 35, top fitch). When the rods are worked out to the butts, piece in two rods (compare Fig. 34), butt to butt (Fig. 35, first or middle fitch), and work out as already described.

(5) Cross fitching is effected by doubling the stakes throughout ; either inserting them down the upsetting (Fig. 36) or down a narrow rand (Fig. 35). The stakes are then separated, crossed and held in position by the first fitch ; the crossing is then reversed (Fig. 35), or, if a shallower basket be desired the border may be laid down above the first fitch (Fig. 36).

(6) For bordering purposes bye-stakes may be cut off immediately before the border is laid down, or they may be laid down in the border (Fig. 5) ; in the case of cross-fitching, they may be laid down with the stake (Fig. 36) or reduced to singles. In the last event care must be taken not to cut off the stakes proper, or the structure of the basket would be fatally weakened. In stout fitched-work such as bottle prickles, cabbage crates, etc., hoop sticks (cleft-hazels) are generally used for bye-stakes, and cut off before bordering.

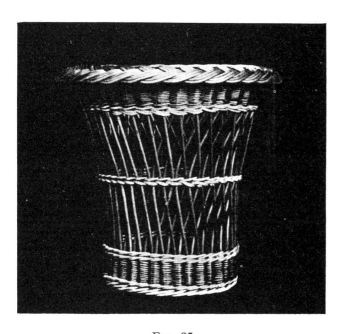

Fig. 35.

Fig. 36.

CHAPTER IX.

(1) THE chief differences to be noted in the methods of Randed work are : that fine White or Buff is normally used, being generally of a better quality than osier; that the sticks and stakes are relatively smaller and closer together, and that, except in cane work, no odd stick or stake is used. Randing is sub-divided into Coarse, Slight, Light, Fine and Close, according to the intervals between the sticks and the stakes and the fineness of the randing.

(2) (a) In *Coarse Randed* baskets, such as Meat Hampers and Railway Truck Baskets, the stakes are set about $2\frac{1}{2}$ in. apart and coarse stout randing is used for siding up.

(3) (b) In *Slight Randed* work, such as Provision Baskets and City Warehouse Baskets, the stakes are set about 2 inches apart and the siding is rather smaller in size.

(4) (c) In *Light Randed* work, such as Soiled-Linen Baskets, Cradles and Doctors' Baskets, the stakes are set about $1\frac{1}{2}$ in. apart with still smaller siding.

(5) (d) In *Fine Randed* work, such as the better quality of Doctors' Baskets, Letter Baskets and Silk Baskets, the stakes are set about 1 or $1\frac{1}{4}$ in. apart and the finest and smallest sizes of stuff are used for siding. In all the above the bottom and cover sticks also vary in their intervals and the randing is not driven very close with the iron ; but in

(6) (e) *Close Randing,* such as is used in Linen Hampers, Travellers' Hampers, Transit Hampers, etc., the siding is driven closely together by blows with the iron and the intervals between the stakes vary from $1\frac{1}{2}$ to $1\frac{3}{4}$ in. according to the size of the basket.

(7) (*f*) In Carriage bodies, Motor bodies, Clothes Flaskets, and other work where smooth surfaces are required both outside and inside, *Tuck or Prick Randing* is used, and each rod of the randing, instead of being simply laid in (Fig. 37), is cut out and tucked in alongside the stake.

(*g*) *Rib-randing* (§ 9) is used in siding up Carriage and Motor bodies, Flaskets, Soiled-Linen Baskets, or other work where it is desirable to break the monotony of a deep space of simple randing. The stakes of randed round or oval work may be set equidistant by the upsetting.

RANDED WORK: ROUND AND OVAL

(8) The bottom of a randed round basket is paired (compare Fig. 36) and requires no odd stake. Fig. 37, of which the first round of upsetting consists of a four-rod wale, will illustrate the method of simple randing. Before the siding up is begun the handful of randing necessary to carry up the basket to its required depth is first carefully drafted into four or five graded sizes. Embracing the stuff loosely within his left arm, or standing it in a tub or " belly," the worker first draws out the longest rods which he lays at his right side, he then draws out the next longest which he lays at right angles to the first draft, and so proceeds until he has reached the shortest and last draft, being careful to lay each draft across the others so as not to mix them. Having thus prepared his randing, he begins by laying in one of the rods from the last and shortest draft, which rod he works out, alternately in front of and behind one stake, to the end, leaving the top projecting outwards (Fig. 37, to the left). Taking up another rod from the same draft he lays it in, one stake in advance of the butt of the first rod, and works it out in the same manner; thus proceeding he lays in the rods one by one driving the strokes down with his iron

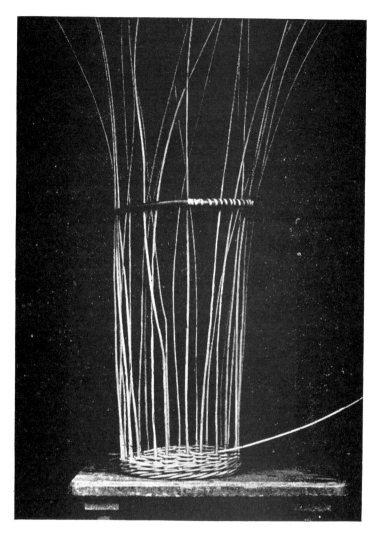

F<small>IG</small>. 37.

as close as the nature of the work demands (Fig. 37). When the first draft is exhausted he starts on the next and so continues until the requisite depth is reached when a wale is put on and the stakes are bordered down.

(9) *Rib-Randing.*—An umbrella or stick basket[1] (Fig. 38) will illustrate this method of randing. The bottom is paired, and, as the basket is to be footed, the upsett is begun with the tops of the waling, which are laid in behind three successive stakes (compare Fig. 57). The upsett is not brought down between bottom-stick and stake, since the foot-rods have to be inserted subsequently alongside the stakes. Having completed our upsett—in this case three rounds of waling—and drafted our siding, we take the first rod alternately in front of two and behind one stake for two strokes, and then work it out as in simple randing. The second, and all subsequent rods, are laid in and carried for the first two strokes in front of two stakes and behind one in an exactly similar manner. This will give the randing the rib-like aspect seen in the illustration. Having randed the basket up to one-fourth of its intended height, this first section is cut off by a five-rod wale, and then for a second section the side is randed up with cane pith in continuous ribbing, *i.e.*, each and every stroke is taken alternately in front of two stakes and behind one, another hank of cane being pieced in as the former is exhausted. Two alternate rands must be used to prevent overlapping, since the stakes are even. A second five-rod wale is now worked in, and a third section, in cane pith, in ribbed randing, follows ; this in its turn being terminated by a third five-rod wale, and the siding completed by a fourth and last section of rib-randing in willow. In this section I have widened the ribbing by taking an extra turn, each rod being carried in front of two and behind one stake

[1] The illustrations are not intended as models ; I have made them solely to illustrate methods.

thrice before being worked out in simple randing. During the whole of the siding-up the iron will be in use closing down the randing. Four rounds of four-rod waling are now put on, and the stakes are bordered down behind two and in front of four.

(10) The tops of the stakes will now serve as foot-rods. Having cut them out and reversed the basket, a foot-rod is inserted alongside each stake, the slype inwards (dip the ends first in the shop-pot), a hole being made with the bodkin if necessary. The foot-rods are held in position by two rounds of waling ;[1] they are then laid down as for a border, the foot is levelled by blows with the iron, and the tops are cut off and laid aside for future use (compare Fig. 5). The basket, except for picking, is completed. All forms of ribbing may be carried out in willow or in cane, and are applied to oval and square work as well as round.

(11) *Borders.*—The ordinary and the running borders (Figs. 12 and 14) may be used with effect for fine work, and it will be obvious to the alert pupil that each method will lend itself to many variations. In the former (Fig. 12) we may lay down three, four, five or six stakes and carry the strokes in front of two, three, four or five stakes or the stakes may be laid down behind two (Figs. 5 and 17) instead of one. In the latter method (Fig. 14), the first and each successive stake may be laid down in front of or behind two and then worked out ; or the ends of the rods, which should project outwards, may be neatly finished off with a Plait, or a Track after the manner of a Tracked cover (see Fig. 48).

(12) *The Plaited Border.*—A more complicated but more pleasing border is that known as the plaited border which is admirably adapted for fine work, but demands

[1] They may also be sprung outwards a couple of inches with three or four rounds of waling so that the basket shall stand more firmly.

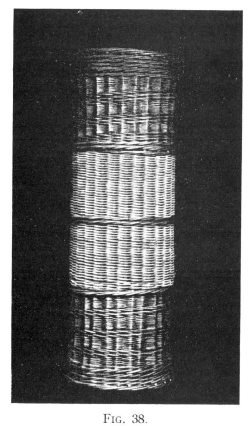

Fig. 38.

good, tough, kind willow for its carrying out. Begin by numbering nine stakes consecutively. Double the first five ; lay down three of these double stakes in succession towards you ; loop the first of them rather loosely over the second and third, and lay it in between the fourth and the fifth, with the tops away from you. Lay down the fourth double stake over it and towards you ; then loop the second double stake over the third and fourth and lay it between the fifth and sixth, *i.e.*, between the last double and the first single stake.[1] Lay down the fifth double stake over that just turned in ; take up the third double, loop it over the fourth and fifth and lay it between the sixth and seventh stakes. You will now have three double stakes—the first, second and third —laid down away from you. Take up the first of these, bring it towards you over the second and third, and lay it between the sixth and seventh ; then lay down the sixth stake (the first single one) towards you and alongside it ; you will now have a triple lying towards you preceded by two doubles. Take up the first of these doubles, loop it over the next and over the triple—and lay it between the seventh and eighth stakes. Then take up the first of the three doubles now lying away from you, bring it over the second and third, and then towards you between the seventh and eighth stakes. Lay down the seventh alongside it, thus forming a second triplet ; take up the fifth double—the last to your left—loop it over the two triplets and lay it between the eighth and the ninth stakes. Bring back the first of the three doubles lying away from you and lay down the eighth stake alongside it. You will thus have three triplets towards you (Fig. 39).[2] Drop the inner member of the

[1] It will facilitate the finishing of the border if the first stroke is held down by a peg placed underneath the second, and the second in like manner held down by a peg under the third.

[2] For clearness the stakes have been cut away and loosened in the illustration ; in practice they should be thumbed tightly in.

first of these and lay the other two members between the ninth and tenth stakes.   Thus continue, working alternately in front of three and behind two stakes (always dropping the inner member of each triplet), until the point where the border was begun ; then with the aid of the bodkin draw each stroke into its appropriate

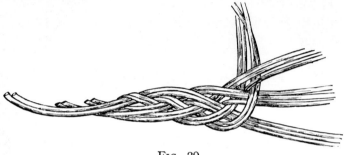

Fig. 39.

place in the plait and cut off the projecting tops.   The finishing strokes will be distinguished at the bottom of Fig. 40 (where I have carried out this border in cane pith) by the series of five quadruple turns indicating the places where the last strokes have been drawn in.   The projecting tops, before they are cut off, may be turned over and caught up, each by each in succession, and then cut off (Fig. 44).

(13) Many variations of this form of border will also suggest themselves to the alert and ingenious worker. Two (Fig. 41) or four (Fig. 42) double stakes may be laid down at the beginning instead of three, or the inside strokes may be brought behind three instead of two stakes ; or the whole series of stakes may be doubled (Fig. 36, willow) and the border begun with triple instead of double stakes.

(14) *The Rope Border.*—This, a modification of the plaited border, may be carried out by numbering six stakes in succession and doubling the first two.   Lay

FIG. 40.

Fig. 41.

FIG. 42.

FIG. 43.   FIG. 44.

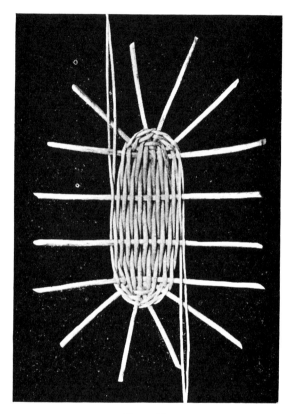

FIG. 45.

down the first of these towards you, giving the two members a rope-like turn on themselves, then lay it inside between the second and third stakes. Lay down the second double, giving it a similar turn, and lay it inside between the third and fourth stakes. Bring back the first double towards you, lay down No. 3 with it and, giving the three members a rope-like turn, lay them inside between the fourth and fifth stakes. Bring back a second double, lay down No. 4 with it and, giving a similar turn, lay between the fifth and sixth stakes. You will now have two triplets lying away from you ; dropping the lower member of the first (which member has now done its work) bring back the other two members, lay down No. 5 with them, and so continue until the point of commencement has been reached ; then draw the finishing strokes in to their appropriate places and cut off projecting tops. To broaden the border the beginning may be made by inserting three or four extra rods and extra members thus added to the strokes throughout (Fig. 43).

(15) *The Cover Border.*—The cover of a randed basket, round or oval, is also made on the same method as the bottom and paired up. No odd stick is required (Fig. 45), but an extra cover-stick will generally be desirable, especially if the belly be flowed ; and a neater finishing than is afforded by a pair may be effected by a border. Having paired or randed the cover up to within half an inch of the required size, cut off the ends of the sticks close to the work and insert border-rods, rather smaller than stakes, alongside and to the left of each stick ; then, without reversing the cover, proceed to turn down two rods in succession—the first behind the second, the second behind the third, bringing the tops toward you. Take up the first rod, lay it behind the fourth, and turn down the third alongside it. Then continue the border until it is completed, cramming the last strokes

in, or, if cane be used, drawing them through to their proper places. See Fig. 46, where I have applied this form of finishing a cover to a cane-pith basket. The tracked border (§ 16) may also be applied to round as well as to oval covers (Fig. 47, upper, and Fig. 48).

(16) *Tracking.*—Having cut out border-rods, insert one alongside and to the *right* of each cover stick. Beginning at the back (*i.e.*, where the ties are to go), and *without* reversing the cover, lay down each border rod in succession behind two and in front of one, leaving the rods turned back away from you ; then finish this first stage of the work by drawing the last rods through into their appropriate places. This done, reverse the cover, again beginning at the back, and, having prepared two rods to piece in, proceed to lay down the track. Number the projecting rods 1 to 7. Take up No. 1, and lay it rather loosely (or peg it down to allow of the last strokes being drawn in) behind No. 2 and let it lie in front of No. 3. Lay down No. 2 behind No. 3 and let it lie in front of No. 4. Double No. 1 by piecing in an extra rod in front of it, then lay these two in front of No. 3, behind No. 4 and let them lie in front of No. 5. Lay down No. 3 alongside these two and piece in the second extra rod alongside and in front of No. 2 ; lay these two in front of No. 4 and behind No. 5, and let them lie in front of No. 6. Lay down No. 4 alongside them. Take up the first two[1] (the third, No. 1, has done its work) of the three to your left, lay them in front of No. 5 and behind No. 6, and let them lie in front of No. 7. Lay down No. 5 alongside them, and so continue the track, dropping the furthest of the three rods to your left at each stroke, until the point is reached at which the track was begun, when, drawing in each rod to its appropriate place, the track

---

[1] Or the three may be taken up (compare Fig. 25), the rod (one of four) dropped at the next stage, and the track thus broadened.

FIG. 46.

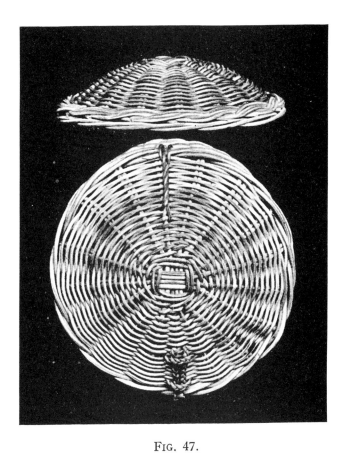

FIG. 47.

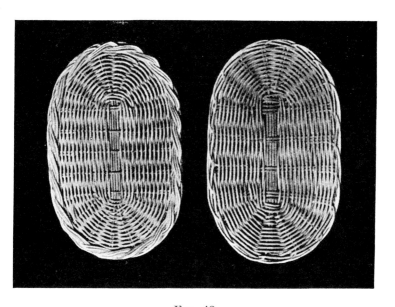

FIG. 48.

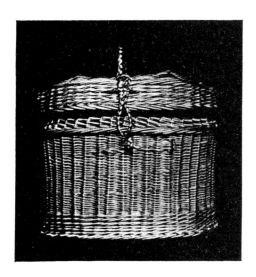

FIG. 49.

is completed and the projecting ends of the rods are cut off.

In Fig. 47 (top), and Fig. 48, I have applied the track to a round and two oval covers in cane-pith ; in Fig. 48, the lower cover illustrates the first stage of the track as seen from the inside (concave) of a cover ; the upper, the outside (convex) of a tracked cover.

(17) *Ties, Hasps and Nooses.*—The cover has now to be tied on and this may be neatly done by a modification of the band (Fig. 32), two (or three) of the turns being taken through the cover and under the border. See Fig. 47, where I have applied this method to a basket in cane pith. The band thus serves two purposes : that of a hinge, and that of a band which prevents the border of the cover from drawing.

(18) *Trunk Covers.*—A trunk cover (Fig. 49) may be made to any form of basket by sett'ng the stakes inwards when the proper depth has been reached.   This is effected by a stout four or five rod wale, then a neck of one or two inches is formed by a running border or by two or three rounds of pairing and a narrow ordinary border (frontispiece). The cover is then carefully carried out to its due proportion and staked up, the stakes being pricked up without reversing the cover, which then, treated as a bottom, is upsetted and waled up to the depth necessary to fit well over the neck ; it is finished by being bordered off in any form of close narrow border (Fig. 49).

CHAPTER X.

A METHOD OF MAKING ROUND AND OVAL WORK, ADAPTED FOR WOMEN WORKERS.

(1) ROUND and oval bottoms and covers may be made in a sitting position. This method, largely practised in Continental village industries, is admirably adapted for women workers in willow or cane-pith, although the writer has known women home-workers in willow who

FIG. 50.

practised the more masculine method and successfully competed with men in making the long narrow, oval fish baskets formerly used at Billingsgate and known as Alligators.

(2) For round work, one set of bottom-sticks instead of being laid *over* is run *through* the other, each member of which is pierced by the bodkin or knife in the middle (Fig. 50). If the bottom is of fine willow and for a

fitched or randed basket, no odd stick or stake will be needed and the slath may be begun with the tops of the slath-rods (Fig. 36) and the bottom paired up ; if it is to be slewed the slath should be opened out as in Fig. 7, or, if cane is to be used, the odd stick may be formed by inserting an extra half stick (Fig. 51). The hank of cane

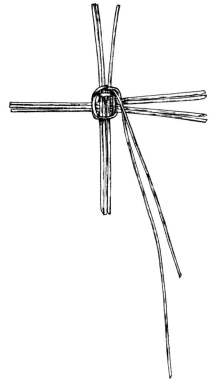

FIG. 51.

should be carefully selected for the slath, there being considerable difference in the density of cane, both whole and pith ; the softer and kinder hanks should therefore be set aside for slathing, upsetting, fitching and similar

purposes. There should also be a difference of at least
two sizes between slathing and bottom-sticks, and indeed
for beginners a much wider interval is advisable ; or
relatively stout willow sticks may be used, following the
workshop practice for heavy cane work. There should
also be a decurrent interval of two sizes or more between
bottom-sticks and stakes, and between stakes and siding.
Let us apply the method to cane pith work.

(3) Having chosen our cane for slathing, one end of
which should be left shorter than the other and carry
so far only as the opening out of the sticks, we tie the

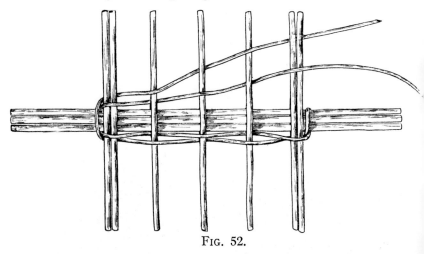

FIG. 52.

slath by one (or two) successive turns, and then proceed
to open out the sticks, first in pairs and then singly (Fig.
51); if twelve sticks are. used, open out first in threes.
When the sticks are all opened out, one end of the slathing
is dropped (Fig. 53) and the bottom randed up to its size.

(4) For oval work, varying numbers of short and long
sticks are used, the latter are run through the former (Fig.
52), and the slath opened out as in Fig. 54, or, if skeins are
used, the short sticks may be run through the long, and

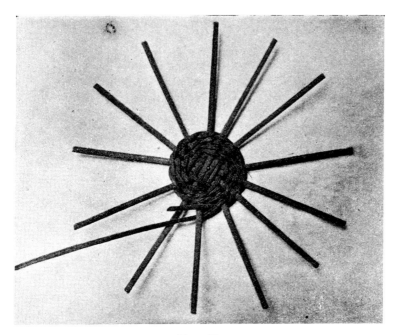

FIG. 53.

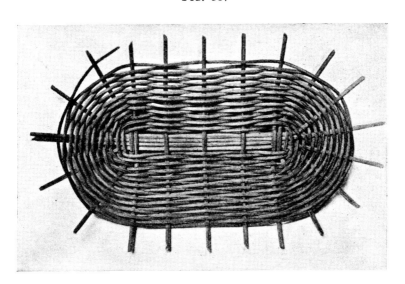

FIG. 54.

Fig. 55.

held in position by crossing the skein over each stick or pair of sticks as they are laid in, and lapping it round the intervals. The short sticks may, of course, be doubled (compare Fig. 48). It will be noted (*a*) that the shoulders and ends of the slath only are paired, the sides being randed in alternate strokes, and (*b*) that the odd stick, if one be needed, is relegated to the end.

(5) In Fig. 55 I have made up Fig. 54 into a small arm-basket, using thirty-seven stakes. The element of waste is a serious one, especially when cane is used, and the worker should carefully estimate the length of the stakes when cutting them out. He must estimate for (*a*) insertion in the bottom, (*b*) depth of the side, (*c*) laying down of the border, allowing an inch or so of margin. With long practice this is effected empirically by the eye without measurement, but, if the beginner should have over-estimated the length, the ends of the stakes, when cut off after bordering, should be neatly tied with a piece of cane (Fig. 56) and laid aside for future uses such as piecing borders, footing, and other similar purposes. The hoop method of holding stakes in position is not well adapted for cane work ; opposite stakes may be held to the hoop by ties, or the stakes may be tied together and the hoop discarded, while the first two rounds or more of the upsett are put on.

(6) In some shops where the planks are laid close together the willow worker tops his stakes, but the method is a wasteful one and should, if possible, be avoided. Leagues, except for cudgel-baskets and others not intended to stand erect, are not adapted for cane work, since the reduced proportion of substance between bottom stick and stake cannot be maintained (p. 54) owing to the uniformity of the diameter of a rod of cane as compared with the tapering form of the willow rod. The infirm nature of some cane-pith work, which will not stand firmly and on its bottom, is often due to the neglect

of the necessary relative proportion of size in the material used for the various parts.

(7) The basket staked and slewed up (Fig. 55) to the required size, is bordered off, either with an ordinary or a plaited border.[1] A piece of whole cane or stout willow will be required for the bow and the handling should consist of cane, relatively smaller than in the case of the twisted willow (Fig. 27) since the material has a pull similar to that of the untwisted willow. A larger number of turns over the bow will therefore be required and the handling will be taken thrice under the border at each side (Fig. 55). A tie should be made across the basket with a set in the opposite direction to the pull of the handling, and kept on while the basket is drying. A handle made on this method will never draw, whatever weight may be carried in the basket.

(8) The outward pressure of the bow against the sides may be counteracted by soaking the bow before the basket is begun, then turning it to the required curve of the handle, holding it in position with a tie and hanging it up to dry ready for use.

[1] Owing to the greater flexibility of cane the last strokes of the ordinary border may be drawn through into their respective positions and not crammed in.

FIG. 56.

FIG. 57.

CHAPTER XI.

(1) In setting about the bottom of a randed square basket it will be necessary to employ a larger number of sticks than is required for a slewed bottom, varying them in number, however, with the relative fineness of the randing. The same choice of stout outside sticks is imperative, or the outside sticks may be doubled. In all square work the smaller tops of the sticks may be used up for inside sticks by doubling them.

(2) In randed work (as also in finer slewing) the side stakes are driven through the outside stick, holes at regular intervals through the stick being made with the staking-bodkin by blows with the mallet.

(3) If the corners are to be blunt, as in Fig. 57, the stouter corner stakes are inserted a short space from the actual corner of the bottom, as in the slewed basket (Fig. 31). If the side stakes are of even number the two centre stakes are driven in next after the corner stakes : if odd, the centre stake is thus treated, and the spacing of the remaining stakes facilitated.

(4) The waling of the upsett will be begun at each side, tops first, if the basket is to be footed, and not pulled down over against the bottom (Fig. 57, where the foot has been removed).

(5) Begin the randing at the side intended to serve for the back (Fig. 57), having first inserted four dry liners at the corners, butts upwards, immediately after two rounds of the upsett have been completed. Finish the siding with a top wale, and if end handles are required they should be put on before the border is laid down (Fig. 57).

(6) In randing up the cover, spaces should be marked, or lightly notched, on the outside stick where the two holes for the ties are to be turned, such spaces to correspond with intervals between stakes in the back of the basket.　The randing of the cover at these holes may be either turned round the stick next to the outside or, if the interval be too wide, a small stick may be inserted to carry the randing and thus avoid the gap which in the former method would be seen between the outside stick and the next one (Fig. 57).

(7) A neater cover-border to the ends will be necessary than that used for the slewed cover.　This is formed by inserting border rods, beginning with two at the left-hand outside stick, and cramming the last two strokes in at the right-hand stick (Fig. 57).　The corners are blunted by taking a couple of turns of the randing round the sticks next the outside ones (Fig. 57) before the border is laid down.　The corners will now be banded by four long bands to prevent the borders drawing.

(8) The cover is tied on with cane or twisted willow ties in the simple manner shown in the illustration, the end of the tie being either taken a turn or two along the side randing (Fig. 57, left), or taken round the butt and behind two turns of the tie below the border (Fig. 57, right).

(9) If the basket is designed to meet hard wear the foot may be of cane, or, if not footed, the first round of the upsett may be of cane.

(10) *Square corners* instead of blunt are used for certain work (Fig. 58).　In staking up a basket of this form, the first stakes are set a little further away from the corners ; the four corner sticks are cut from stout two-yearling, dry rods, and slyped and notched where they are to lie against the corner of the bottom ; the upsett is begun at the ends, each corner stick being held in position by the waling of the upsett as shown in the illustration (Fig. 58).

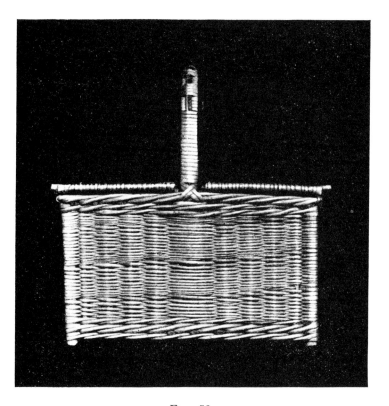

Fɪɢ. 58.

Skill and practice are needed to keep the corners square and true.

(11) A slight modification of the ordinary border may be made at the corners. After the top wale has been put on, the corner sticks should be cut off level with it and replaced by stakes which are driven down the centre of each stick with the aid of the bodkin. The border shown is laid down in the ordinary manner behind two and in front of three stakes. When the stake next before the corner is reached, instead of being laid down behind two, this stake is laid down behind one—the inserted corner stake—together with the preceding stake. It is then dropped and does no more work. The next rod to be taken up is held over against the corner stake and the following rod held against and in front of it ; the third rod is then turned sharply and firmly over these two in front of the corner stake (Fig. 58), and laid in behind the stake next the corner. The outer rod lying against the corner stake is now brought forward in front of the corner stake and the stake next following it, and laid in behind the second stake from the corner. The corner stake is then laid down beside it, and the second of the rods left at the corner is brought forward and laid in behind the third stake from the corner. The border is carried out in the normal manner until the next corner is reached, when the modified process is repeated.

If the corners are not thus squared two stakes may be inserted, one each side of the stick, and the corners blunted as in Fig. 57.

(12) *Cross Handles and Bridged Covers.*—If the basket is to be carried on the arm, even stakes should be used for the sides and the two central stakes left open for the bow rod as in the oval slewed basket (Fig. 27). If it is to be covered as well as cross-handled, each of the ends should have an odd stake ; then, after the border has been

laid down, a bridge is carried across from side to side before the liners are withdrawn (p. 73).

(13) *The Bridge.*—Two stout rods are inserted at each side of the liners and randed up to the width of the basket, when they are crammed down on the opposite side. The handle is now put on (p. 144) and the bridge held in position by the crossed skeins of the handle, which pass under the border and through the bridge (Fig. 59).

(14) Two covers are now made on hoops and an even number of scalloms, the tongues of the scalloms being turned away from the centre to begin the formation of the hole, which is then completed by being randed up backward and forward on each side after the manner shown (Fig. 59). A wale is next carried across the whole width of the cover, and the randing continued until the requisite length has been reached, when the scalloms are bordered down behind one and in front of two. The covers are tied on to the bridge by two long bands (compare Fig. 47), and an eye (Fig. 59) is made corresponding to the hole in the cover at each end, by turning the butt of a rod round the bodkin, sharpening the ends, and driving them down alongside the middle stake. A sharp, dry peg is next cut and driven, with the aid of the bodkin, through them and the stake to prevent the eye drawing. One turn of the wale of the cover is then lifted carefully with the bodkin to take the tongue of the loose pin that holds the cover in position (Fig. 59). This bridged cover is also applicable to blunt-cornered square baskets and to oval baskets. The same methods are applied to square work in cane, and scalloms are also used in that material.

Fig. 59.

CHAPTER XII.

SKEIN HANDLES—PREPARATION OF SKEINS.

(1) EXCEPT for Flat Skein work, a purely local industry, skeins are chiefly used by the ordinary basket-maker for handling, and for siding up light work, such as Letter Baskets, Picnic Baskets, Soiled-Linen Baskets, etc. ; the old-fashioned reticule, of which no less than twenty-seven sizes and styles are specified for the last time in the London Basket-makers' List of 1850, has long been hustled out of the market by cheap and showy foreign substitutes, largely the product of sweated industry.

(2) The process of making skeins is fairly simple with the tools at the disposition of the civilised worker, who has not, as the primitive craftsman had, to rely on his teeth and a sharp flint. Taking a three or four-way cleave (Fig. 3, *g* and *h*) and choosing a tough, fine, dry willow, Long-Skin for preference—he tops it a few inches, starts the cleavage (three or four way) with his knife ; then holding the rod in the left hand, he inserts the cleave with his right and pushes it downwards to the butts, carefully guiding it so that the skeins are uniformly cloven.

(3) He then takes up the shave (Fig. 3 (*k*)) and, setting the knife of it by the screw to the appropriate level, he draws the skein, pith upwards, against the knife, holding the skein in position by pressure of the left thumb (which may be protected by a leather thumbstall), thus shaving off the central wood of the skein ; setting the knife to a narrower level he repeats the process until the skein is evenly and finely shaven from top to butt. The work of the shave is now done, and for the coarser forms of skein work no further preparation (except dipping in water) is needed.

(4) For finer work the upright (Fig. 3 (*l*)) comes into use. Having set the pair of knives to the requisite width, the skein, held in position by the left thumb, is drawn against them skin upwards, from top to butt, and so made uniform in width.

(5) Skeins of cane (chair cane) are bought already prepared, but, for coarser handling, whole cane is split in two, and shaved by being drawn against the shop knife held on the knee.

(6) *Lapped Skein Handles.*—Two (or three) bow rods of dry willow or cane are needed, and are inserted (butt and top, if willow) down opposite sides. Skeins, duly up-righted, having been prepared, a watered willow or cane leading-rod should be selected of sufficient length to lead over the bow rods, allowing a margin of length of about 6 or 8 inches. This leading-rod (shown in Fig. 60 in front of the two bow-rods) is slyped like a scallom, the tongue run up under the front of the border and between it and the bow-rods. The rod is then brought up in front of the border and laid over against the bow-rods (the leading-rod may be of cane of double length and carried across double, Fig. 59) ; a skein is inserted alongside and to the left of the bow-rods, lapped diagonally once or twice over the leading rod and under the border holding it firmly in position (Figs. 58 and 59). The skein is then lapped simply round the leading and bow-rods, from left to right, for a few inches, and taken alternately under and over the leading-rod, as shown in Figs. 58 and 59, fresh skeins being pieced in (see under-side of handle, Fig. 59) as required.

(7) When the arc of the bow has been thus alternately lapped over to within 3 or 4 inches of the opposite border, the end of the leading-rod is run under the front of the border as at the beginning ; the simple lapping is then resumed down to the border and the skein lapped diagonally across leading-rod and border, making an exact

replica of the strokes at the beginning of the handle. The skein is then drawn in and out of the work along the side and cut off.

(8) If the basket is designed to carry a heavy weight, this handle may be strengthened by driving a sharp peg of dry willow through stakes and bow-rods at each side immediately under the border, or between the waling (Fig. 58).

(9) It will be obvious that many variations may be made in carrying out the lapping ; it may be alternated in uniform single, double and triple turns ; it may be taken once over and twice under the leading-rod, or the reverse ; or it may be taken thrice over and twice under, and so varied almost indefinitely.

(10) *Listed Skein Handles.*—In Fig. 42, a flower basket of cane pith, I have carried out a listed handle with skeins of ordinary chair cane and a rod of whole cane for a leading-rod. The skein, having been lapped round bow and leading-rod for a few inches, as in the former handle, is taken for three turns alternately and singly over and under the leading-rod (Fig. 60), then dropped for a while, and, three listing skeins having been prepared, long enough to carry over the whole handle, one of them is inserted alongside and to the right of the leading-rod where the simple lapping ends, brought over across to the left and laid under the leading-rod and in front of the dropped skein. This dropped skein is now picked up, lapped once over and under the tie and again dropped. The second listing skein is inserted just above the first and, like it, brought over and across to the left and laid under the leading-rod. The dropped lapping-skein is again picked up, lapped over and under the leading-rod and dropped. The third listing skein is now inserted above the second and brought over and across and laid under the leading-rod, the lapping-skein being yet again lapped over and under the leading-rod. The three listing

skeins and the one lapping skein will now be lying to the right (Fig. 60). This alternate lapping and listing is continued until the simple lapping is to be resumed, when the leading rod is slyped and its tongue brought under the border as in the former handle. The ends of the listing skeins are now cut off, caught up in the simple lapping, and the handle is finished in the usual way.

(11) Variations in this form of handle will also suggest themselves to the intelligent worker ; the listing skeins may be reduced to one or two, or increased to four or more, or the two methods of simple lapping and listing may be combined (Fig. 44). This handle should also be pegged if applied to a basket designed to carry a heavy weight.

Fig. 60.

CHAPTER XIII.

HASPS AND NOOSES (PLAITED).

(1) THE hasp and noose is largely used in basket-work for fastening covers, and is adapted for a padlock or a pin or a bar. The noose or nooses should be worked in before the border is laid down or the top wale put on (frontispiece). Two carefully selected, fine rods are needed for the noose, the larger of which is topped to the length required for two members of the plait with a few inches margin for finishing. This is turned at the middle round the bodkin, to prevent kinking, and then drawn through and on each side of the appropriate stake which, if a single hoop and noose is to be applied, should be preferably a central stake[1] in the front of an oval or square basket, or, in a round basket, opposite where the tie is to go (Fig. 46). The noose being plaited from below upwards, the first rod is drawn through about an inch or so down the randing and the second rod inserted alongside and gripped by it. The three members of the plait being now present are plaited up ; the noose is turned upward and the ends of the plaiting are taken round the stake and then worked in for a turn or two in a reverse direction along the top of the randing. The top wale is now put on and the border laid down.

(2) The hasp is made after the cover has been tied on. Three fine rods are needed, and, having been cut out and topped, are inserted alongside a stick, either the outside one or the next to it, with the aid of the bodkin. They are then plaited to the required size of the loop which is formed by drawing one of the rods through an opposite

---

[1] If the centre is a pair of stakes, it may be inserted between them and held against an inserted slip of willow or cane (Fig. 48).

member of the plait with the aid of the bodkin (Fig. 57).
The plait rods are then drawn through the cover, two of
them are twisted, brought back through the cover and
turned over the beginning of the plait ; they are then
drawn through the turn inside the cover and cut off.
A neater finish may be given by beginning the plait
higher up the cover and, after the loop has been formed,
plaiting the rods out for some inches and taking two turns
with the plait over and under the cover before the ends
are drawn through the inside turns and cut off (Figs.
46, 47). The cover of a square basket may also be
fastened by turning two holes through the front of the
cover (corresponding to the holes for the ties) through
which two plaited eyes fixed on the border project. A
long stick or bar runs through the eyes and fastens the
cover, which may be fitted with a double-rod handle
taken round the central stick of the cover; or, if the
cover-sticks are even, round a short stick laid inside the
cover.

(3) The plaited hasp and noose may be applied to cane
pith work (Figs. 46, 47), and is indeed often made of cane
in ordinary willow work for greater durability. If cane
is used, the first two members of the hasp may be formed
of one long rod of cane drawn through each side of the
cover-stick (Fig. 47).

Conclusion.

Such are the chief principles and methods that should
govern the craft of basket-making in its simpler aspects.
There is little of conscious design in the art ; most of its
forms are traditional, and, once the necessary sleight of
hand and mastery of material have been acquired, small
difficulty will be found in making the varied articles of
wicker-work in common use. I do not therefore propose
to illustrate them by models and descriptions. Obviously
the coarser and heavier work must be made by men,

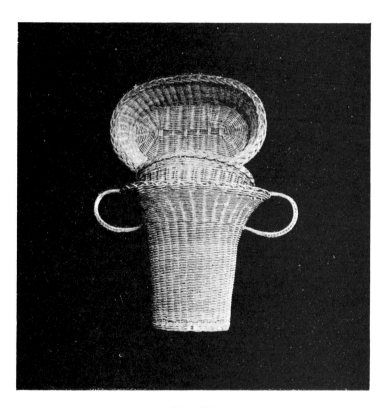

FIG. 61.

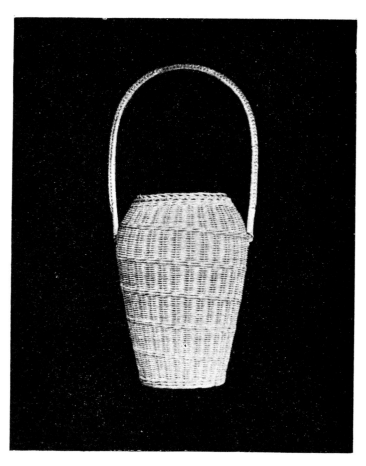

FIG. 62.

demanding, as it does, considerable physical strength, especially of fingers and wrist, and a position of the body ill-adapted for women workers. There is, however, a field open for the exercise of women's skill, invention and artistic sense in meeting the demand for the lighter kinds of ware, such as work-baskets, reticules, flower-baskets, hand-baskets, bicycle baskets, waste-paper baskets, etc., a demand now largely met by cheap, showy, flimsy, foreign importations. Based on the traditional and more durable methods of the English craftsman, a fair range of variation both in design and treatment is possible in the production of such articles—I have suggested possibilities by Figs. 43, 61 and 62 (F.g. 44 is by a Leicester workman)—and, if but the English consumer can be educated to respond, a lost branch of native handicraft may be recovered. But the art must be regarded as a serious business of life, to be thoroughly learned and strenuously practised, and not as another of the feeble, feminine digital activities by which vacuous hours may be whiled away.

Glossary of Technical Terms.

Back.—The convex side of a willow rod (Fig. 6, C).

Band.—A rod of willow or cane which binds the finishing pair, or track, or cram, or border of a cover to the fabric of the same and prevents the finishing strokes from drawing ; much used in repairing (p. 83 § 16 ; Figs. 26, 32). Combined with tie (Figs. 47, 59).

Belly.—(*a*) The concave side of a willow rod (Fig. 6, D) ; also applied to (*b*) a bordered basket ready for the cover (p. 80 § 15).

Border.—The finishing strokes of the body (belly) of a basket ; also applied to covers (p. 20 § 2 ; Fig. 5 ; pp. 34-45 §§ 10, 11 and Figs. 12-15 ; pp. 96-121 §§ 11-16 and Figs. 36, 39, 40, 41, 43, 44, 46, 47, 48, 58 ; p. 130, note).

Bow-rod.—A rigid arc of willow or cane which forms the core of a cross handle (p. 68 § 9 ; p. 73 § 10).

Bridge.—A narrow piece of randing carried across a basket on which the covers are swung (p. 139 §§ 12, 13 and Fig. 59).

Butt.—The thick end of a willow rod (Fig. 6, B).

Bye-stakes.—Supplementary stakes inserted after upsetting (p. 20 § 2, and Fig. 5 ; p. 84 § 2).

Cram.—A sharpened, turned-down stake used in the finishing strokes of a border (p. 38 and Fig. 13).

Fitch.—Two rods of willow or cane worked alternately under and over each other and gripping a stake or bye-stake at each stroke (p. 20 § 2 and Fig. 5 ; pp. 84-86 and Figs. 33, 34, 35, 36).

Foot.—The raised border worked on to the bottom of a basket on which it stands (p. 23 § 2 ; Fig. 5).

Handle.—(*a*) *Single.* A handle made from one rod of willow or cane (p. 45 § 12).
(*b*) *Double.* A handle made from two rods of willow or cane (p. 45 § 13).
(*c*) *Cross.* A handle made from a bow or bows with turns taken round or lapped over them (p. 73 § 10 ; p. 130 § 7).

Hank.—A length of cane bent up in the middle before it is tied into a bundle (p. 123).

Hasp.—Plaited rods of willow or cane wrought on to the cover of a basket to drop over a noose worked in the front (p. 149 § 2 ; Figs. 46, 47, 49).

Hoop.—(*a*) A contrivance for holding the stakes temporarily in position (p. 26 § 5 and Fig. 37).
(*b*) The rigid outer frame of a cover or bottom on which the scalloms are laid (p. 75 § 11 and Fig. 28).

Lapping.—The act of binding skeins round bow-rods, or sticks, or a core of any material used for basket-making (p. 129 § 4 ; p. 144 §§ 6-9 ; Figs. 58, 59).

Leading-rod.—A rod of willow or cane carried over a lapped cross handle and gripping the border at each side (p. 144 § 6 ; Figs. 59, 60).

League.—A continuous bottom-stick and stake (p. 54 § 1 and Fig. 21).

Liners.—Dry rods of willow or cane inserted alongside stakes (p. 73 § 9).

Listing.—An additional skein or skeins worked in with the lapping of skein handles (p. 145 § 10 ; Figs. 42, 60).

Noose.—Plaited rods of willow or cane worked on the front of a basket under the top wale, over which a hasp on the cover falls (p. 149 § 1 ; Figs. 46, 49 and Frontispiece).

Osier.—(*a*) Specifically *Salix viminalis ;* often used to denote all kinds of willows cultivated for basket-making.
(*b*) The coarse, full-topped, as distinguished from the fine-topped, varieties of willow (p. 6 § 1).

Pair.—Two rods of willow or cane worked alternately over and under each other—the reverse of a fitch (p. 20 § 2, and Fig. 5).

Picking.—Cutting off the projecting ends of rods when the work is partially or wholly finished (p. 28 § 6 ; p. 96 § 10).

Pricking up.—Turning up the stakes after their insertion in the bottom with the point of the shop-knife to form the framework of the sides of a basket (p. 20 § 2, and p. 28 § 7).

Rand.—A single rod of willow or cane worked alternately in front of and behind the stakes (p. 20 § 2 and Fig. 5 ; Sub-divisions of, pp. 91, 92 §§ 1 to 7).

Rods.—(*a*) A comprehensive term applied by the basket-maker to all willows used in his craft.
(*b*) Also applied to lengths cut from a hank of cane for basket-making purposes.

Scallom.—A method of forming the rigid inner frame of a bottom or cover, or of staking up a basket (p. 75 § 11 and Fig. 28 ; p. 79 § 14 and Fig. 32).

Skein.—A strip of the outer skin of willow or cane (p. 143 §§ 2-5).

Slath.—The tying together and opening out of the bottom or cover sticks of a round or oval basket (p. 20 § 2 and Fig. 5 ; p. 25 § 4, Figs. 7 and 8 ; p. 54 § 2 ; pp. 122-9 §§ 2-4).

Slew.—Two or more rods of willow or cane worked together alternately in front of and behind the stakes (p. 20 § 2 and Fig. 5 ; p. 33 § 9 and Fig. 11).

Slype.—A long cut (p. 25 § 2 and Fig. 6, F and E ; Fig. 29).

Stakes.—Rods of willow or cane inserted in the bottom of a basket and pricked up to form the rigid framework of the sides (p. 20 § 2 and Fig. 5 ; p. 28 § 7 and Fig. 10 ; p. 135 §§ 2, 3).

Sticks.—(*a*) Topped willows of two or more years' growth. (*b*) Short lengths of any willow or cane cut out for a bottom or cover.

Stroke.—Any complete movement in basket-work : analogous to a stitch in needlework.

Tie.—(*a*) The turns on which the cover of a basket swings (p. 60 § 7 and Fig. 26 ; p. 83 § 17 and Fig. 57 ; p. 136 § 8). (*b*) A temporary band across a basket to counteract the pull of a cross handle (p. 74 and p. 130, § 7).

Top.—The upper end of a willow rod (Fig. 6, A).

Track.—A method of finishing off covers (p. 112 § 16) or borders (p. 96 § 11).

Trunk Cover.—A deepened cover which fits over the border or neck of a belly and rests on the top wale (p. 121 § 18, Fig. 49).

Upsett.—Two, three, or more rods of willow or cane worked alternately on the stakes immediately they are pricked up in order to set them firmly in position (p. 20 § 2 and **Fig.** 5 ; p. 33 § 8).

Wale.—Three or more rods of willow or cane worked alternately, one by one, in front of two, three, or more stakes, and behind one (p. 20 § 2 and Fig. 5).